AAT

Qualifications and Credit Framework (QCF)

AQ2013

LEVEL 3 DIPLOMA IN ACCOUNTING

TEXT

Accounts Preparation

2015 Edition

For assessments from September 2015

Third edition June 2015
ISBN 9781 4727 2167 9

Previous edition
ISBN 9781 4727 0901 1

British Library Cataloguing-in-Publication Data
A catalogue record for this book is available from the British
Library

Published by
BPP Learning Media Ltd
BPP House
Aldine Place
London
W12 8AA

www.bpp.com/learningmedia

Printed in the United Kingdom by Martins of Berwick
Sea View Works
Spittal
Berwick-Upon-Tweed
TD15 1RS

Your learning materials, published by BPP Learning Media Ltd, are
printed on paper obtained from traceable sustainable sources.

CONTENTS

A NOTE ABOUT COPYRIGHT

BPP LEARNING MEDIA'S AAT MATERIALS

The AAT's assessments fall within the **Qualifications and Credit Framework** and most papers are assessed by way of an on demand **computer based assessment**. BPP Learning Media has invested heavily to ensure our materials are as relevant as possible for this method of assessment. In particular, our **suite of online resources** ensures that you are prepared for online testing by allowing you to practise numerous online tasks that are similar to the tasks you will encounter in the AAT's assessments.

Resources

The BPP range of resources comprises:

- **Texts**, covering all the knowledge and understanding needed by students, with numerous illustrations of 'how it works', practical examples and tasks for you to use to consolidate your learning. The majority of tasks within the texts have been written in an interactive style that reflects the style of the online tasks we anticipate the AAT will set. When you purchase a Text you are also granted free access to your Text content online.

- **Question Banks**, including additional learning questions plus the AAT's sample assessment(s) and a number of BPP full practice assessments. Full answers to all questions and assessments, prepared by BPP Learning Media Ltd, are included. Our question banks are provided free of charge online.

- **Passcards**, which are handy pocket-sized revision tools designed to fit in a handbag or briefcase to enable you to revise anywhere at anytime. All major points are covered in the Passcards which have been designed to assist you in consolidating knowledge.

- **Workbooks**, which have been designed to cover the units that are assessed by way of computer based project/case study. The workbooks contain many practical tasks to assist in the learning process and also a sample assessment or project to work through.

- **Lecturers' resources**, for units assessed by computer based assessments. These provide a further bank of tasks, answers and full practice assessments for classroom use, available separately only to lecturers whose colleges adopt BPP Learning Media material.

This Text for Accounts Preparation has been written specifically to ensure comprehensive yet concise coverage of the AAT's **AQ2013** learning outcomes and assessment criteria.

Each chapter contains:

- Clear, step by step explanation of the topic

- Logical progression and linking from one chapter to the next

- Numerous illustrations of 'how it works'

- Interactive tasks within the text of the chapter itself, with answers at the back of the book. The majority of these tasks have been written in the interactive form that students can expect to see in their real assessments

- Test your learning questions of varying complexity, again with answers supplied at the back of the book. The majority of these questions have been written in the interactive form that students can expect to see in their real assessments

The emphasis in all tasks and test questions is on the practical application of the skills acquired.

Supplements

From time to time we may need to publish supplementary materials to one of our titles. This can be for a variety of reasons, from a small change in the AAT unit guidance to new legislation coming into effect between editions.

You should check our supplements page regularly for anything that may affect your learning materials. All supplements are available free of charge on our supplements page on our website at:

www.bpp.com/about-bpp/aboutBPP/StudentInfo#q4

Customer feedback

If you have any comments about this book, please email nisarahmed@bpp.com or write to Nisar Ahmed, AAT Head of Programme, BPP Learning Media Ltd, BPP House, Aldine Place, London W12 8AA.

Any feedback we receive is taken into consideration when we periodically update our materials, including comments on style, depth and coverage of AAT standards.

In addition, although our products pass through strict technical checking and quality control processes, unfortunately errors may occasionally slip through when producing material to tight deadlines.

When we learn of an error in a batch of our printed materials, either from internal review processes or from customers using our materials, we want to make sure customers are made aware of this as soon as possible and the appropriate action is taken to minimise the impact on student learning.

As a result, when we become aware of any such errors we will:

1) Include details of the error and, if necessary, PDF prints of any revised pages under the related subject heading on our 'supplements' page at: www.bpp.com/about-bpp/aboutBPP/StudentInfo#q4

2) Update the source files ahead of any further printing of the materials

3) Investigate the reason for the error and take appropriate action to minimise the risk of reoccurrence.

A NOTE ON TERMINOLOGY

The AAT AQ2013 standards and assessments use international terminology based on International Financial Reporting Standards (IFRSs). Although you may be familiar with UK terminology, you need to now know the equivalent international terminology for your assessments.

The following information is taken from an article on the AAT's website and compares IFRS terminology with UK GAAP terminology. It then goes on to describe the impact of IFRS terminology on students studying for each level of the AAT QCF qualification.

Note that since the article containing the information below was published, there have been changes made to some IFRSs. Therefore BPP Learning Media have updated the table and other information below to reflect these changes.

In particular, the primary performance statement under IFRSs which was formerly known as the 'income statement' or the 'statement of comprehensive income' is now called the 'statement of profit or loss' or the 'statement of profit or loss and other comprehensive income'.

What is the impact of IFRS terms on AAT assessments?

The list shown in the table that follows gives the 'translation' between UK GAAP and IFRS.

UK GAAP	IFRS
Final accounts	Financial statements
Trading and profit and loss account	**Statement of profit or loss (or statement of profit or loss and other comprehensive income)**
Turnover or Sales	Revenue or Sales Revenue
Sundry income	Other operating income
Interest payable	Finance costs
Sundry expenses	Other operating costs
Operating profit	Profit from operations
Net profit/loss	Profit/Loss for the year/period
Balance sheet	**Statement of financial position**
Fixed assets	Non-current assets
Net book value	Carrying amount

UK GAAP	IFRS
Tangible assets	Property, plant and equipment
Reducing balance depreciation	Diminishing balance depreciation
Depreciation/Depreciation expense(s)	Depreciation charge(s)
Stocks	Inventories
Trade debtors or Debtors	Trade receivables
Prepayments	Other receivables
Debtors and prepayments	Trade and other receivables
Cash at bank and in hand	Cash and cash equivalents
Trade creditors or Creditors	Trade payables
Accruals	Other payables
Creditors and accruals	Trade and other payables
Long-term liabilities	Non-current liabilities
Capital and reserves	Equity (limited companies)
Profit and loss balance	Retained earnings
Minority interest	Non-controlling interest
Cash flow statement	**Statement of cash flows**

This is certainly not a comprehensive list, which would run to several pages, but it does cover the main terms that you will come across in your studies and assessments. However, you won't need to know all of these in the early stages of your studies – some of the terms will not be used until you reach Level 4. For each level of the AAT qualification, the points to bear in mind are as follows:

Level 2 Certificate in Accounting

The IFRS terms do not impact greatly at this level. Make sure you are familiar with 'receivables' (also referred to as 'trade receivables'), 'payables' (also referred to as 'trade payables'), and 'inventories'. The terms sales ledger and purchases ledger – together with their control accounts – will continue to be used. Sometimes the control accounts might be called 'trade receivables control account' and 'trade payables control account'. The other term to be aware of is 'non-current asset' – this may be used in some assessments.

Level 3 Diploma in Accounting

At this level you need to be familiar with the term 'financial statements'. The financial statements comprise a 'statement of profit or loss' (previously known as an income statement), and a 'statement of financial position'. In the statement of profit or loss the term 'revenue' or 'sales revenue' takes the place of 'sales', and 'profit for the year' replaces 'net profit'. Other terms may be used in the statement of financial position – eg 'non-current assets' and 'carrying amount'. However, specialist limited company terms are not required at this level.

Level 4 Diploma in Accounting

At Level 4 a wider range of IFRS terms is needed, and in the case of Financial statements, are already in use – particularly those relating to limited companies. Note especially that a statement of profit or loss becomes a 'statement of profit or loss and other comprehensive income'.

Note: The information above was taken from an AAT article from the 'assessment news' area of the AAT website (www.aat.org.uk). However, it has been adapted by BPP Learning Media for changes in international terminology since the article was published.

ASSESSMENT STRATEGY

Duration

The Accounts Preparation (ACPR) assessment is a two hour assessment.

This unit is about students having the required skills and knowledge to prepare ledger accounts to trial balance stage according to current financial standards, including making any necessary adjustments. Learners will know how to account for the purchase and disposal of non-current assets.

Competency

Students will be assessed as competent if at least 70 per cent of the available marks are achieved in the assessment. The level descriptor in the table below describes the ability and skills students at this level must successfully demonstrate to achieve competence.

QCF Level descriptor	**Summary**
	Achievement at Level 3 reflects the ability to identify and use relevant understanding, methods and skills to complete tasks and address problems that, while well defined, have a measure of complexity. It includes taking responsibility for initiating and completing tasks and procedures as well as exercising autonomy and judgment within limited parameters. It also reflects awareness of different perspectives or approaches within an area of study or work.
	Knowledge and understanding
	■ Use factual, procedural and theoretical understanding to complete tasks and address problems that, while well defined, may be complex and non routine
	■ Interpret and evaluate relevant information and ideas
	■ Be aware of the nature of the area of study or work
	■ Have awareness of different perspectives or approaches within the area of study or work
	Application and action
	■ Address problems that, while well defined, may be complex and non-routine
	■ Identify, select and use appropriate skills, methods and procedures
	■ Use appropriate investigation to inform actions
	■ Review how effective methods and actions have been
	Autonomy and accountability
	■ Take responsibility for initiating and completing tasks and procedures, including, where relevant, responsibility for supervising or guiding others
	■ Exercise autonomy and judgment within limited parameters

Task types

These will include:

- Completion of ledger accounts
- Completion of pro-forma tables
  - Non-current assets register
  - Journal
  - Trial balance
  - Extended trial balance
- Calculations
- Multiple choice or similar

Accounts Preparation (APR) is the first of two financial accounting assessments at Level 3. It is recommended that ACPR is studied and taken before FSTP.

The ACPR assessment consists of six independent tasks, all of which should be attempted. Students will normally be assessed by computer-based assessment. Students' 'own figures' will be taken into account whenever possible. For this reason, and to achieve maximum marks, students should always try to offer answers for all parts of a task.

Students will be assessed as competent if at least 70 per cent of the available marks are achieved in the assessment.

The assessment – what it will cover

Maintaining accounting records for non-current assets

Tasks will include accounting for acquisitions, disposals and depreciation:

- The non-current assets register
- Ledger accounts relating to non-current assets transactions

Accounting adjustments and reconciliations

Typical tasks will require accounting for period end adjustments and the correction of errors. This will include using:

- Ledger accounts
- The extended trial balance
- The journal
- Short answer questions
- Reconciliation of control accounts (sales, purchases) with subsidiary accounts
- Reconciliation of bank account (cash book) with bank statement

Principles, concepts and records

Tasks will include:

- Showing basic understanding of accounting framework and concepts
- Showing understanding of the principles of double entry bookkeeping
- Showing awareness of the different types of accounting records, and their purpose

The trial balance and extended trial balance

Tasks will include:

- Production of a trial balance (or partial trial balance) from ledger accounts
- Completion of an adjusted extended trial balance

AAT UNIT GUIDE

Accounts Preparation (ACPR)

Introduction

Please read the information below in conjunction with the QCF standards for the unit.

This is a Level 3 unit concerned with accounting principles and concepts, accounting for non-current assets and advanced bookkeeping to final adjusted trial balance stage.

It integrates with a number of other units in the qualification, all concerned with financial accounting. At Level 2, Processing bookkeeping transactions (PBKT) and Control accounts, journals and the banking systems (CJBS) introduce students to basic bookkeeping skills and the books of original entry. At Level 4, Financial statements (FSTM) prepare students to produce financial statements for limited companies. The two Level 3 units, ACPR and Prepare final accounts for sole traders and partnerships (FSTP) form a bridge between Level 2 basic bookkeeping and Level 4 higher level financial accounting skills. Together they cover the theoretical foundations of financial accounting, as well as practical skills for the preparation of financial statements for unincorporated traders.

It is recommended that this unit is taken before FSTP. ACPR and FSTP are derived from the NOS FA-4, Prepare Accounts.

The purpose of the unit

ACPR is the first of the two Level 3 financial accounting units. Covering accounting principles and concepts, accounting for non-current assets and advanced bookkeeping, it takes the student from Level 2 foundation knowledge and skills and prepares them for further development in FSTP where they will be preparing financial statements for sole traders and partnerships.

A business organisation employing a student who has been successful in these two units will have a member of the accounting team who can work with little supervision. This student could be expected to take bookkeeping to final trial balance and prepare draft financial statements for unincorporated traders.

Terminology

Students should be familiar with IFRS terminology. Other terms are used here to match titles provided by the QCF.

Learning objectives

After completion of this unit, the student will have a good understanding of the accounting principles and concepts that underlie all financial accounting. Having developed a fuller understanding of the accounting equation, they will understand the nature and importance of the different categories of account and how the books and record relate to each other. This will enable them to perform more advanced bookkeeping functions such as accounting for non-current assets and accounting for adjustments and they will recognise the importance of reconciling control accounts. Finally they will use the extended trial balance to account for adjustments and extract a profit or loss figure for the period.

Learning outcomes

The unit consists of eight learning outcomes. The learner will:

1. Understand generally accepted accounting principles and concepts

2. Understand the principles of double entry bookkeeping

3. Understand the accounting methods used to record non-current assets

4. Account for the purchase of non-current assets

5. Account for depreciation

6. Account for the disposal of non-current assets

7. Account for adjustments

8. Prepare and extend the trial balance

There are a number of assessment criteria linked to each learning outcome and these have been incorporated into the delivery guidance under the appropriate topics. Those referenced K relate to knowledge and those referenced S relate to skills.

Learning Outcome	Assessment Criteria	Covered in Chapter
1 Understand generally accepted accounting principles and concepts	1.1K Explain the accounting principles of going concern, accruals, prudence and consistency.	2
	1.2K Explain the purpose of maintaining financial records for internal and external use.	1
	1.3K Describe the types of accounting records that a business should maintain and the main uses of each.	1
	1.4K Describe the main requirements of accounting standards (IFRS) in relation to inventory and non-current asset valuations.	3, 7
	1.5K Explain the accounting characteristics of relevance, reliability, comparability, ease of understanding and materiality.	2
	1.6K Explain the differences between capital and revenue expenditure, classifying items as one or the other.	3
2 Understand the principles of double entry bookkeeping	2.1K Explain the accounting equation.	1
	2.2K Define assets, liabilities and equity in an accounting context.	1
	2.3K Explain the purpose and use of books of prime entry and ledger accounts.	1
	2.4K Explain the purpose of reconciling the sales and purchases ledgers, and the cash book.	9, 10
3 Understand the accounting methods used to record non-current assets	3.1K Describe how the acquisition of non-current assets can be funded, including part exchange.	3
	3.2K Explain the accounting treatment for recording the acquisition and disposal of non-current assets.	3, 5
	3.3K Explain the need for, and methods of, providing for depreciation on non-current assets.	4
	3.4K Describe the contents and use of the non-current assets register.	3
	3.5S Resolve any queries, unusual features or discrepancies relating to the accounting records for non-current assets or refer to an appropriate person.	5

Learning Outcome	Assessment Criteria	Covered in Chapter
4 Account for the purchase of non-current assets	4.1S Calculate total capital expenditure including all associated costs.	3
	4.2S Record prior authority for the capital expenditure.	3
	4.3S Record in the appropriate accounts the acquisition of a non-current asset including funded by part exchange.	3
	4.4S Record the acquisition in a non-current assets register.	3
	4.5S Close off or transfer the ledger account balances at the end of the financial period.	3
5 Account for depreciation	5.1S Calculate the depreciation charges for a non-current asset using the: • Straight line method • Reducing (diminishing) balance method	4
	5.2S Record the depreciation in the non-current assets register.	4
	5.3S Record depreciation in the appropriate ledger accounts.	4
	5.4S Close off the ledger accounts at the end of the financial period, correctly identifying any transfers to the statement of profit or loss.	4
6 Account for the disposal of non-current assets	6.1S Identify the correct asset, removing it from the non-current assets register.	5
	6.2S Record the disposal on non-current assets in the appropriate accounts.	5
	6.3S Calculate any gain or loss arising from the disposal, closing off or transferring the account balance.	5

Learning Outcome	Assessment Criteria	Covered in Chapter
7 Account for adjustments	7.1K Explain the accounting treatment of accruals and prepayments to expenses and revenue.	6
	7.2K Explain the reasons for, and method of, accounting for irrecoverable debts and allowances for doubtful debts.	8
	7.3S Record the journal entries for closing inventory.	7
	7.4S Record the journal entries for accrued and prepaid expenses and income.	6
	7.5S Record the journal entries for provision for depreciation, irrecoverable debts and allowances for doubtful debts.	4, 8
	7.6S Record the journal entries to close off revenue accounts in preparation for the transfer of balances to the final accounts.	11
8 Prepare and extend the trial balance	8.1S Prepare ledger account balances; reconciling them, identifying any discrepancies and taking appropriate action.	11
	8.2S Prepare a trial balance.	11
	8.3S Account for these adjustments: ■ Closing inventory ■ Accruals and prepayments to expenses and income ■ Provisions for depreciation on non-current assets ■ Irrecoverable debts ■ Allowance for doubtful debts	11
	8.4S Prepare the trial balance after adjustments.	12
	8.5S Check for errors and/or inaccuracies in the trial balance, taking appropriate action.	12

1. Understand generally accepted accounting principles and concepts

1.1K Explain the accounting principles of going concern, accruals, prudence and consistency

- Recognise the definitions of the underlying assumptions of the accrual basis and the going concern basis

- Recognise when the accruals basis of accounting has been applied, for example depreciation charges, allowance for doubtful debts, accruals and prepayments, closing inventory

- Recognise circumstances when a business is no longer a going concern and understand the effect this has on the value of its assets

- Recognise the terms consistency and prudence; however prudence will not be explicitly tested as it is not encouraged in the IFRS Framework

1.2K Explain the purpose of maintaining financial records for internal and external use

- Internal control

- Measuring business performance

- Obtaining credit/financing

- Statutory requirements

- Understand the importance of keeping financial records physically secure

- Understand when it is appropriate to restrict access to financial records, and why

- Students should be aware of the content and purpose of an income statement and a statement of financial position, although the requirement to prepare these statements is in unit L3FSTP

1.3K Describe the type of accounting records that a business should maintain and the main uses of each

- Non-current assets register
- Books of prime entry: day books, cash book and journal
- General ledger accounts
- Subsidiary ledger accounts: purchases and sales
- Inventory records

1.4K Describe the main requirements of accounting standards (IFRS) in relation to inventory and non-current asset valuations

IAS 2 *Inventories*

- Understand that inventory must be valued at the lower of cost and net realisable value, on an item by item basis

- Understand how to calculate net realisable value and apply this to given data

- Recognise that unit cost, FIFO and weighted average cost are acceptable valuation methods but LIFO is not. Calculations of valuations on these bases will not be required

- Understand what can be included in the cost of inventory:

  - Cost of purchase, including delivery
  - Cost of conversion including direct labour

- Understand what cannot be included in the cost of inventory:

  - Storage costs of finished goods
  - Selling costs

- Recognise the link with the accruals basis, ie the cost of inventory is recognised in the income statement when the goods are sold

IAS 16 *Property, Plant and Equipment*

- Recognise the term property, plant and equipment

- Understand the terms useful life, residual value, depreciable amount, carrying amount

- Recognise the need for depreciation charges and have a basic understanding of the purpose of depreciation (including a link with the accruals basis)

- Understand what can be included in cost:

  - Cost of purchase, including delivery
  - Cost of construction, including own labour costs
  - Cost of site preparation, including own labour costs
  - Cost of testing
  - Professional fees

- Understand what cannot be included in cost:

  - Repair, maintenance and servicing costs
  - Administration and general overheads

- Finance costs and staff training costs will not be tested

- Recognise that depreciation methods should be reviewed regularly (but not including circumstances in which methods may or may not be changed)

- Impairments or revaluations will not be tested

1.5K Explain the accounting characteristics of relevance, reliability, comparability, ease of understanding and materiality

- Scope is based on the IFRS Framework

- Recognise that in order to be useful, financial information should have two fundamental characteristics:

  - Relevance. Understand that materiality is an aspect of relevance specific to individual organisations

  - Faithful representation

- Recognise that the following characteristics support relevance and faithful representation:

  - Comparability
  - Verifiability
  - Timeliness
  - Understandability

- Students will need to recognise the terms and have a basic understanding of their meaning. Detailed explanation or application of the terms will not be expected

1.6K Explain the differences between capital and revenue expenditure, classifying items as one or the other

- Understand the importance of materiality in deciding whether to capitalise

- Understand the relevance of the useful life of the purchase in deciding whether to capitalise

- Understand the relevance of the accruals basis; how and why the capital expenditure is charged to the income statement over time rather than at the time of purchase

- Discriminate between capital expenditure and revenue expenditure in the context of the organisation in question by correctly applying any given capitalisation policy

2. Understand the principles of double entry bookkeeping

2.1K Explain the accounting equation

- Recognise its importance in an effective double-entry bookkeeping system

- Recognise and explain how elements of the equation are affected by a range of accounting transactions

2.2K Define assets, liabilities and equity in an accounting context

- Equity will be referred to as capital in the context of sole traders and partnerships

- Understand and apply the meanings of assets, liabilities and capital, including

- Non-current assets and current assets

- Tangible and intangible assets

- Current liabilities and non-current liabilities

- Basic understandings of what an intangible asset is and recognise goodwill as an intangible asset (IAS 38 is beyond the scope of this unit)

2.3K Explain the purpose and use of books of prime entry and ledger accounts

- Day-books, cash book, journal, general (main, nominal) ledger accounts

- Recognise the books of prime entry

- Describe the type of information that is recorded in each of the various records

- Understand how the accounting records relate to each other

2.4K Explain the purpose of reconciling the sales and purchases ledgers, and the cash book

- As external verification of correct bank balance
- To find errors, including omissions
- Understand that reconciliations may not show all errors

3. Understand the accounting methods used to record non-current assets

3.1K Describe how the acquisition of non-current assets can be funded, including part exchange

- Cash purchase (this includes standard commercial credit terms, for example 30 days)

- Part exchange

- Borrowing. Recognising the terms (loans, hire purchase, finance lease), but detailed knowledge of accounting treatment of these is not required

- Identify the suitability of particular funding methods in the context of a given simple business situation

3.2K Explain the accounting treatment for recording the acquisition and disposal of non-current assets

- Understand how to calculate depreciation charges for non-current assets acquired or disposed of during an accounting period in accordance with the policies of the organisation

- Be able to complete the disposal account

3.3K Explain the need for, and methods of, providing for depreciation on non-current assets

- Understand the purpose of depreciation and the relevance of the accruals basis, ie to allocate the depreciable amount over the asset's useful life

- Understand how to choose an appropriate method of depreciation, i.e. straight line or diminishing balance, according to the pattern of usage expected over the asset type's useful life

- Understand how to choose an appropriate rate of depreciation, i.e. the percentage or fraction, according the length of the asset type's expected useful life

3.4K Describe the contents and use of the non-current asset register

- As internal control, to include verification of physical assets and/or general ledger accounts

- Identify data types that would be appropriately included or not included in the register

3.5S Resolve any queries, unusual features or discrepancies relating to the accounting records for non-current assets or refer to an appropriate person

- Understand that non-current asset register, non-current asset accounts and/or physical check may not correspond

- Identify a reasonable explanation for any differences

4. Account for the purchase of non-current assets

4.1S Calculate total capital expenditure including all associated costs

- Identify directly attributable costs that can be included in the cost of capital expenditure when non-current assets are acquired, in accordance with the relevant accounting standards (IAS 16)

- Identify revenue expenses that should not be included in the cost of capital expenditure when non-current assets are acquired

- Understand how to treat VAT charged on capital expenditure, according to the VAT registration status of the organisation

- Finance costs will not be tested

4.2S   Record prior authority for the capital expenditure

- Understand why authorisation is necessary for an organisation

- Identify the appropriate person to provide authorisation for a given organisation

4.3S   Record in the appropriate accounts the acquisition of a non-current asset including funded by part exchange:

Accounts that may be tested:

- Non-current asset at cost account – (for example, motor vehicles, machinery)

- Bank/cash account

- Loan account (finance costs will not be tested)

- Disposals

4.4S   Record the acquisition in a non-current assets register

- Make the appropriate entries in accordance with the organisation's given policies and procedures

Funding methods:

- Cash purchase (including standard commercial credit terms, eg 30 days)

- Part exchange

- Loan

- HP and finance leases – awareness only, no accounting entries or technical knowledge required

4.5S   Close off or transfer the ledger account balances at the end of the financial period

- Understand which accounts will have balances carried forward and which are closed off to the income statement at the end of the financial period

- Understand that revenue or expense accounts will carry a balance prior to the closing off to the income statement at the end of the financial period

5. Account for depreciation

5.1S Calculate the depreciation charges for a non-current asset using the

- Straight line method

- Reducing balance method

- Reducing balance method to be referred to as Diminishing balance method

- Calculate depreciation in accordance with the given policies of the organisation

- Straight line method, using a percentage, fraction or over a period of time, including cases when there is expected to be a residual value. Pro-rata calculations for part of a year will be required only when the organisational policy stipulates

- Diminishing balance method using a percentage. Pro-rata calculations for part of a year will not be required

5.2S Record the depreciation in the non-current assets register

- Make the appropriate entries in accordance with the organisation's given policies and procedures

5.3S Record depreciation in the appropriate ledger accounts

- Non-current asset accumulated depreciation account (eg motor vehicles, machinery)

- Depreciation charges account

5.4S Close off the ledger accounts at the end of the financial period, correctly identifying any transfers to the statement of profit or loss

- Understand which accounts will have balances carried forward and which are closed off to the income statement at the end of the financial period

- Understand that revenue or expense accounts will carry a balance prior to the closing off to the income statement at the end of the financial period

6. Account for the disposal of non-current assets

6.1S Identify the correct asset, removing it from the non-current asset register

- Understand that the carrying amount of an asset that has been disposed of will always be shown as zero at the end of the period

6.2S Record the disposal of non-current assets in the appropriate accounts

- Non-current asset at cost account – (eg motor vehicles, machinery)

- Non-current asset accumulated depreciation account – (eg motor vehicles, machinery)

- Non-current asset disposals account (or just Disposals account)

- Bank/cash account

6.3S Calculate any gain or loss arising from the disposal, closing off or transferring the account balance

7. Account for adjustments

7.1K Explain the accounting treatment of accruals and prepayments to expenses and revenue

- Recognise a given account as an income or expense type

- Understand the terms accrued expenses, accrued income, prepaid expenses, prepaid income

- Understand the significance of these at the period beginning and end and the link to the accruals basis

- Understand how opening and closing accruals and prepayments affect income and expense ledger accounts, including recognition of the reversal of a previous period adjustment

- Know that adjustments may need to be calculated pro-rata

- Know how to calculate the amount transferred to the income statement at the end of the period, including recognition that this is not necessarily the amount paid/received in the period

7.2K Explain the reasons for, and method of, accounting for irrecoverable debts and allowances for doubtful debts

- Recognise and explain the link to the accruals basis

- Know how to account for irrecoverable debts written off, allowances for specific doubtful debts and general allowances for doubtful debts

- Recognise the recovery of a debt previously written off as irrecoverable

- Excluding VAT implications

7.3S Record the journal entries for closing inventory

- Calculate correct closing inventory figure in accordance with the relevant accounting standards (IAS 2). This may include calculating the cost from selling price including VAT and/or an element of profit

- Use closing inventory account – statement of profit or loss (SPL)

- Use closing inventory account – statement of financial position (SFP)
- Journal narratives may be required

7.4S Record the journal entries for accrued and prepaid expenses and income

- Calculate adjustments pro-rata using given information, including organisational policies. Prepare journal entries for these adjustments
- Journal narratives may be required
- Reversal journals will not be required
- Journal postings may be tested by the use of ledger accounts showing accrued and prepaid expenses and income at the beginning and/or end of the period

7.5S Record the journal entries for provision for depreciation, irrecoverable debts and allowances for doubtful debts

- Calculate a new allowance for doubtful debts according to a given policy – specific and/or general
- Calculate the adjustment to an existing allowance (increase or decrease) according to a given policy
- Correctly use the following accounts:
  - Non-current asset accumulated depreciation account (SFP)
  - Depreciation charges account (SPL)
  - Irrecoverable debts account (SPL)/Sales ledger control account (SFP)
  - Allowance for doubtful debts account (SFP)
  - Allowance for doubtful debts adjustment account (SPL)

7.6S Record the journal entries to close off revenue accounts in preparation for the transfer of balances to the final accounts

- Account types may be income or expense
- Journal narratives may be required

8.   Prepare and extend the trial balance

8.1S Prepare ledger account balances, reconciling them, identifying any discrepancies and taking appropriate action

- Sales ledger control account to sales ledger; adjustments may be required to either or both balances
- Purchases ledger control account to purchases ledger; adjustments may be required to either or both balances

- Bank account to bank statement; including an understanding that a debit entry or balance in the ledger will be a credit on the statement, and vice versa. Familiarity with banking terms such as BACS, direct debit etc will be expected

- Discriminate between items that affect the reconciliation and those that do not

- Correct ledger accounts by journal or show adjustment in ETB

8.2S Prepare a trial balance

- Transfer balances from ledger accounts, a list of balances or written task data into correct debit or credit column of trial balance

- May require simple adjustments for accruals/prepayments according to given data

8.3S Account for these adjustments

- Closing inventory

- Accruals and prepayments to expenses and income

- Provisions for depreciation on non-current assets

- Irrecoverable debts

- Allowance for doubtful debts

- Use the appropriate columns in the extended trial balance or produce journal entries

8.4S Prepare the trial balance after adjustments

- Accurately extend figures in the ledger balances and adjustments columns into the income statement and statement of financial position columns of the extended trial balance

- Recognise that the balancing figure represents the profit or loss for the period, make the entries and label appropriately

8.5S Check for errors and/or inaccuracies in the trial balance, taking appropriate action

- Correct errors creating imbalance and clear the suspense account, including:
  - One-sided entry
  - Entry duplicated on one side, nothing on the other
  - Unequal entries
  - Account balance incorrectly transferred to trial balance

- Correct any errors not revealed by trial balance, including:
  - Errors of principle
  - Errors of original entry
  - Errors of omission
  - Errors of commission
  - Reversal of entries

- Identification or explanation of the type of error will not need to be recalled

- Correct the errors using the journal or the appropriate columns of the extended trial balance

The assessment

Task	Learning outcome	Assessment criteria	Max marks	Title for topics within task range
1	1,3,4,5,6	1.6K 3.1K, 3.4K, 3.5S 4.1S, 4.4S 5.1S, 5.2S 6.1S	18	Non-current assets register
2	1,3,4,5,6,7	1.6K 3.1K, 3.2K, 3.4K, 3.5S 4.1S, 4.2S, 4.3S, 4.5S 5.1S, 5.3S, 5.4S 6.2S, 6.3S 7.6S	17	Ledger accounting for non-current assets
3	7,8	7.1k 8.3S	16	Accounting for accruals and prepayments of income and expenses
4	8	8.1S, 8.2S, 8.3S, 8.4S	19	Prepare a trial balance and reconciliations
5	7,8	7.3S, 7.4S, 7.5S, 7.6S 8.3S, 8.4S, 8.5S	20	Accounting adjustments in extended trial balance (ETB) or journals
6	1,2,3,7,8	1.1K,1.2K,1.3K,1.4K,1.5K 2.1K, 2.2K, 2.3K, 2.4K 3.3K 7.1K, 7.2K 8.2S, 8.3S, 8.4S, 8.5S	20	Extend the trial balance and show knowledge of accounting framework, accounting equation, records, and standards

chapter 1:
ACCOUNTING PRINCIPLES

chapter coverage 📖

In this introductory chapter we describe the types of accounting record that a business should maintain and the main uses of each. This will help to explain the purpose and importance of maintaining financial records for internal and external use. We also cover some accounting principles with which you should be familiar: double entry bookkeeping, the recording of assets, liabilities, income, expenses and capital, and the trial balance.

The topics covered are:

- ✍ The aim of an accounting system
- ✍ Transactions of a business
- ✍ Primary documents for transactions
- ✍ Primary records for transactions: books of prime entry
- ✍ Ledger accounts
- ✍ Principles of double entry bookkeeping
- ✍ Balancing and closing off the ledger accounts
- ✍ Preparing a trial balance

THE AIM OF AN ACCOUNTING SYSTEM

The aim of any business's accounting system is to ensure that all transactions are correctly recorded and can be gathered together for a period in order to prepare a set of financial statements. There are a number of reasons why this is important:

- To ensure that the business can keep track of all its assets and activities, ie to maintain internal control over the business
- To facilitate measurement of the business's performance, ie to know how the business is doing, to spot whether things are going wrong and to take advantage of situations where things have gone right
- To help obtain financing or other forms of credit, ie to be able to show the outside world that the business is strong and is a good investment
- To meet statutory requirements, principally in relation to taxation (all businesses must maintain sufficient records to be able to calculate their taxable income) and company law (not relevant at Level 3)

The details of accounting systems vary across different businesses depending on the structure of each business, its administrative systems and the nature of its operations. However, all accounting systems have the following general elements:

THE ACCOUNTING SYSTEM

TRANSACTIONS

↓

PRIMARY DOCUMENTS

↓

PRIMARY RECORDS:
BOOKS OF PRIME ENTRY

↓

LEDGER ACCOUNTS

↓

RECONCILIATIONS

↓

TRIAL BALANCE

↓

FINANCIAL STATEMENTS

To ensure that all transactions are recorded in the financial records

To ensure transactions have been correctly recorded

To prepare a set of financial statements

TRANSACTIONS OF A BUSINESS

Typical transactions in a business are summarised below:

Cash sales	–	a sale whereby the customer pays at the time of the sale by cash, cheque, credit or debit card
Credit sales	–	a sale which is made but payment is not required from the customer for a specified period of time such as 30 days
	–	the customer then becomes a RECEIVABLE (also known as a DEBTOR) of the business as they now owe money to the business
Sales returns	–	where goods are returned by a customer as they are faulty or not what was ordered
Receipts from credit customer	–	these will be in the form of cheques received in the post or AUTOMATED PAYMENTS paid directly into the business's bank account using BACS (Bankers Automated Credit System)
Cash purchases	–	PURCHASES may be of goods for use in the manufacture of other goods that the business will sell (raw materials), or of goods that are due to be resold by the business (goods for resale)
	–	cash purchases are purchases that are paid for at the time of purchase, by cheque, cash, credit or debit card
Credit purchases	–	a purchase made from a supplier who gives a period of credit so payment is not due for say 30 days
	–	the supplier then becomes a PAYABLE (also known as a CREDITOR) being someone who is due to be paid by the business
	–	both cash and credit purchases may be of services such as phone charges or electricity, in which case they are called EXPENSES
Purchases returns	–	returns of goods to a credit supplier as the goods are faulty or not what was ordered
Payments to credit suppliers	–	these will normally be made by cheque or BACS but may also be made in cash (notes and coin)
Capital expenditure	–	purchase of NON-CURRENT ASSETS (also known as FIXED ASSETS) which are items that are to be used in the business for the long term (this will be considered in more detail in Chapter 3)

Revenue expenditure	–	general everyday purchases and expenses that a business incurs
Petty cash payments	–	most businesses need to make small cash payments, for example paying the window cleaner
Wages and salaries payments	–	nearly all businesses employ people other than the business's owner, so wages/salaries are an important type of payment. Payments also need to be made to HM Revenue and Customs (HMRC) in respect of payroll taxes (PAYE income tax and national insurance or NIC), and pension administrators in respect of pension contributions from employees and from the business as employer

Task 1

K Jones owes your business £1,200. He is | a receivable/a payable | of the business.

PRIMARY DOCUMENTS FOR TRANSACTIONS

For each transaction considered above there will be some form of PRIMARY DOCUMENT to evidence it.

Cash sales	–	either a receipt will be given for the monies received from the customer or the sale will be automatically recorded on a till roll
Credit sales	–	a SALES INVOICE will be issued to the customer showing the details of the goods or services sold, the amount due, the date the amount is due and any other terms such as discounts
Sales returns	–	a CREDIT NOTE is issued to the customer showing the details of the goods returned, the total amount of the goods and the reason for the credit note
Receipts from credit customers	–	the primary document may be the actual cheque received or a REMITTANCE ADVICE NOTE
Cash purchases	–	if a cheque is written for the goods then the primary document will be the CHEQUE BOOK STUB where the details of the amount and the payee will be recorded

Credit purchases	–	a PURCHASE INVOICE will be received from the supplier showing the details of the goods or services purchased, the amount due, the date that the amount is due and any other terms of payment
Purchases returns	–	a credit note will be received from the supplier showing the details of the goods returned, the amount of the credit and the reason for the return of the goods
Payments to credit suppliers	–	these will either be paid for by cheque, so the primary document will be the cheque book stub counterfoil, or by automated payment in which case there will be some form of authorisation to the bank to make the payment, plus remittance advice note
Cash payments	–	these will be made out of the PETTY CASH BOX, a small amount of cash kept on the premises for the purpose of making cash payments, and will only be paid if there is a valid PETTY CASH VOUCHER. Some businesses, such as retailers, may also pay for items out of cash collected from customers. In this case the receipt from the seller is the primary record
Wages and salaries payments	–	the primary record for wages and salaries payments is the PAYROLL, which sets out gross and net pay, statutory and voluntary deductions from pay, and additional expenses for the employer (NIC and pension contributions)

Task 2

When your business returns goods to a credit supplier you would expect to receive an invoice/a credit note/a receipt/a remittance advice note.

PRIMARY RECORDS FOR TRANSACTIONS: BOOKS OF PRIME ENTRY

Each of the different types of primary document will be recorded in its own PRIMARY RECORD or book of prime entry (also called a book of original entry or day book).

Receipts from cash sales	–	whether these are hand-written receipts or the till roll for the day they will be recorded in the Cash received column of the CASH RECEIPTS BOOK
Sales invoices	–	when sent out to customers these are all recorded in the SALES DAY BOOK
Credit notes issued to customers	–	these are recorded in the SALES RETURNS DAY BOOK
Cheques from credit sales	–	the primary document for these in practice is the REMITTANCE ADVICE NOTE from the customer. These are recorded in the Cash received column of the CASH RECEIPTS BOOK
Purchases invoices	–	when received from suppliers these are all recorded in the PURCHASES DAY BOOK
Credit notes received	–	when credit notes are received from suppliers they are recorded in the PURCHASES RETURNS DAY BOOK
Cheque book stubs	–	the details of all cheque payments taken from the cheque book stubs will be recorded in the Bank payments column of the CASH PAYMENTS BOOK
Automated payments	–	the details of receipts by automated payment will be recorded from the customer's remittance advice note in the Bank receipts column of the CASH RECEIPTS BOOK. Automated payments to suppliers will be recorded in the Bank payments column of the CASH PAYMENTS BOOK
Petty cash payments	–	details of petty cash vouchers will be recorded in the PETTY CASH PAYMENTS BOOK. Receipts for cash payments out of cash that was collected in a till are recorded in the Cash payments column of the CASH PAYMENTS BOOK
Wages and salaries payments	–	details from the payroll as the primary document are recorded in the JOURNAL, which is the book of prime entry for payroll transactions and also for non-standard transactions such as writing off bad (irrecoverable) debts, posting opening entries and correcting errors

6

Task 3

The book of prime entry for invoices received from credit suppliers is the
sales day book/the purchases day book/the cash payments book .

LEDGER ACCOUNTS

The totals and details from each of the books of prime entry are then transferred or posted to the general ledger accounts using the principles of double entry bookkeeping, and to the memorandum ledger accounts.

General ledger

The GENERAL LEDGER (also known as the main ledger or nominal ledger) is where there is a separate ledger account for each type of income, expense, asset, liability and capital that the business has. For example, there will be ledger accounts for sales, purchases, receivables, payables and non-current assets to name but a few.

In the general ledger the account for receivables is normally referred to as the SALES LEDGER CONTROL ACCOUNT and the account for payables is normally referred to as the PURCHASES LEDGER CONTROL ACCOUNT.

Memorandum ledger – the sales ledger

In the SALES LEDGER there is a ledger account kept for each individual customer of the business showing precisely how much is owed by that customer and how that amount is made up.

Memorandum ledger – the purchases ledger

In the PURCHASES LEDGER there is a ledger account kept for each individual supplier of the business showing precisely how much is owed to that supplier and how that amount is made up.

Cash book (cash receipts and cash payments books)

In most accounting systems the cash book (made up of the cash receipts book and the cash payments book) is part of the general ledger as well as being a book of prime entry in its own right.

Petty cash book

The petty cash book is used to record both the receipts of cash into the petty cash box and the payments of petty cash vouchers. In most accounting systems the petty cash book (made up of the petty cash receipts book and the petty cash payments book) is part of the general ledger as well as being a book of prime entry in its own right.

Task 4

If you needed to find the details of how much your business owed to a particular supplier, you would consult the general ledger/the sales ledger/the purchases ledger.

PRINCIPLES OF DOUBLE ENTRY BOOKKEEPING

There are three main principles that underlie the practice of recording transactions in a double entry bookkeeping system:

(a) The DUAL EFFECT of transactions – this means that each and every transaction that a business undertakes has two effects on the business

(b) The SEPARATE ENTITY CONCEPT – this means that the owner of a business is a completely separate entity to the business itself

(c) The ACCOUNTING EQUATION will always balance – the accounting equation is:

ASSETS   minus   LIABILITIES   equals   CAPITAL

- **Assets** are items that the business owns

- **Liabilities** are amounts that are owed to other parties

- The **capital** of the business is the amount that is owed by the business back to the owner – remember that under the separate entity concept the owner and the business are completely separate entities for accounting purposes

    - Income increases the business's capital
    - Expenses decrease the business's capital

Obviously it would not be possible in practice to draw up the accounting equation each time that a business makes a transaction. For that reason the dual effect of each transaction is recorded in ledger accounts using double entry accounting.

BPP
LEARNING MEDIA

Rules for double entry

- If there is a payment made out of the bank/cash account then the entry in the bank/cash account is always a credit and therefore the debit must be to some other account

- If there is a receipt into the bank/cash account then the entry in the bank/cash account is always a debit and therefore the credit must be to some other account

- If a business incurs an expense then this is always a debit entry in the relevant expense account

- If a business earns income then this is always a credit entry in the relevant income account

- An increase in assets is always a debit entry

- An increase in liabilities is always a credit entry

- An increase in capital (the amount owed back to the business's owner) is always a credit entry

This can be summarised in the diagram below:

DEBITS	CREDITS
Money into the business	Money out of the business
Increases in:	Increases in:
Expenses	Income
Assets	Liabilities
	Capital

HOW IT WORKS

We will now complete some ledger accounts for a period of trading.

Jenny Fisher has just started trading and has the following transactions for the month of February recorded in her ledger accounts.

1 Feb Paid £12,000 into a business bank account in order to start the business

Debit   Bank/cash account (bank column) – money in
Credit   Capital account

Bank/cash account

Date	Details	Cash £	Bank £	Date	Details	Cash £	Bank £
1 Feb	Capital		12,000				

Capital account

Date	Details	£	Date	Details	£
			1 Feb	Bank/cash	12,000

The 'details' recorded are the other side of the double entry as this helps to follow through the double entry accounting.

1 Feb Paid a cheque for £3,600 as six months' rent on the shop

Debit   Rent account – expense
Credit   Bank/cash account (bank column) – money out

Bank/cash account

Date	Details	Cash £	Bank £	Date	Details	Cash £	Bank £
1 Feb	Capital		12,000	1 Feb	Rent		3,600

Rent account

Date	Details	£	Date	Details	£
1 Feb	Bank/cash	3,600			

1 Feb Buys goods for resale by cheque totalling £680

Debit   Purchases account – expense
Credit   Bank/cash account (bank column) – money out

Purchases account

Date	Details	£	Date	Details	£
1 Feb	Bank/cash	680			

Bank/cash account

Date	Details	Cash £	Bank £	Date	Details	Cash £	Bank £
1 Feb	Capital		12,000	1 Feb	Rent		3,600
				1 Feb	Purchases		680

8 Feb Purchases a computer, to help with preparing the business accounts, for £900 by cheque

Debit   Non-current asset account – computer
Credit   Bank/cash account (bank column) – money out

Non-current asset account – computer

Date	Details	£	Date	Details	£
8 Feb	Bank/cash	900			

Bank/cash account

Date	Details	Cash £	Bank £	Date	Details	Cash £	Bank £
1 Feb	Capital		12,000	1 Feb	Rent		3,600
				1 Feb	Purchases		680
				8 Feb	Non-current asset		900

8 Feb Purchases more goods for resale from T Trainer on credit for £1,000

Debit	Purchases account – expense
Credit	Purchases ledger control account – liability

Purchases account

Date	Details	£	Date	Details	£
1 Feb	Bank/cash	680			
8 Feb	PL control	1,000			

Purchases ledger control account

Date	Details	£	Date	Details	£
			8 Feb	Purchases	1,000

12 Feb Cash takings of £1,380 for the first two weeks are banked (the cost of the goods was £840)

Debit	Bank/cash account (cash column) – money in
Credit	Sales revenue account – income
Debit	Bank/cash account (bank column) – money in
Credit	Bank/cash account (cash column) – money banked

There is no need to know about the cost of the goods sold as in double entry bookkeeping only purchases and sales are recorded; any profit is dealt with at the end of the accounting period when we record purchases held as inventory into the next period (see Chapter 7).

Bank/cash account

Date	Details	Cash £	Bank £	Date	Details	Cash £	Bank £
1 Feb	Capital		12,000	1 Feb	Rent		3,600
12 Feb	Sales revenue	1,380		1 Feb	Purchases		680
12 Feb	Cash		1,380	8 Feb	Non-current asset		900
				12 Feb	Bank	1,380	

BPP
LEARNING MEDIA

Sales revenue account

Date	Details	£	Date	Details	£
			12 Feb	Bank	1,380

17 Feb Sells goods on credit to Jones Stores for £900 (the cost of these goods was £550)

Debit   Sales ledger control account – asset
Credit   Sales revenue account – income

Sales ledger control account

Date	Details	£	Date	Details	£
17 Feb	Sales	900			

Sales revenue account

Date	Details	£	Date	Details	£
			12 Feb	Bank/cash	1,380
			17 Feb	SL control	900

22 Feb Paid £600 to T Trainer by cheque

Debit   Purchases ledger control account – reduction of a liability
Credit   Bank/cash account (bank column) – money out

Purchases ledger control account

Date	Details	£	Date	Details	£
22 Feb	Bank/cash	600	8 Feb	Purchases	1,000

Bank/cash account

Date	Details	Cash £	Bank £	Date	Details	Cash £	Bank £
1 Feb	Capital		12,000	1 Feb	Rent		3,600
12 Feb	Sales revenue	1,380		1 Feb	Purchases		680
12 Feb	Cash		1,380	8 Feb	Non-current asset		900
				12 Feb	Bank	1,380	
				22 Feb	PL control		600

25 Feb Received cheque for £700 from Jones Stores

Debit	Bank/cash account (bank column) – money in
Credit	Sales ledger control account – reduction of an asset

Bank/cash account

Date	Details	Cash £	Bank £	Date	Details	Cash £	Bank £
1 Feb	Capital		12,000	1 Feb	Rent		3,600
12 Feb	Sales revenue	1,380		1 Feb	Purchases		680
12 Feb	Cash		1,380	8 Feb	Non-current asset		900
25 Feb	SL control		700	12 Feb	Bank	1,380	
				22 Feb	PL control		600

Sales ledger control account

Date	Details	£	Date	Details	£
17 Feb	Sales revenue	900	25 Feb	Bank/cash	700

26 Feb Cash takings of £1,560 for the last two weeks are banked (the cost of the goods that were sold is estimated to be £950)

Debit	Bank/cash account (cash column) – money in
Credit	Sales revenue account – income
Debit	Bank/cash account (bank column) – money in
Credit	Bank/cash account (cash column) – money banked

Bank/cash account

Date	Details	Cash £	Bank £	Date	Details	Cash £	Bank £
1 Feb	Capital		12,000	1 Feb	Rent		3,600
12 Feb	Sales revenue	1,380		1 Feb	Purchases		680
12 Feb	Cash		1,380	8 Feb	Non-current asset		900
25 Feb	SL control		700	12 Feb	Bank	1,380	
26 Feb	Sales revenue	1,560		22 Feb	PL control		600
26 Feb	Cash		1,560	26 Feb	Bank	1,560	

Sales revenue account

Date	Details	£	Date	Details	£
			12 Feb	Bank/cash	1,380
			17 Feb	SL control	900
			26 Feb	Bank/cash	1,560

26 Feb Withdrew £1,200 for her own living expenses

Debit Drawings account – reduction in the liability of capital
Credit Bank account – money out

Drawings are quite a tricky one to remember. Capital is the amount that is owed back to the owner and is therefore a credit balance. Drawings are effectively reducing the amount of capital owed to the owner so they must be a debit entry.

Drawings account

Date	Details	£	Date	Details	£
26 Feb	Bank/cash	1,200			

Bank/cash account

Date	Details	Cash £	Bank £	Date	Details	Cash £	Bank £
1 Feb	Capital		12,000	1 Feb	Rent		3,600
12 Feb	Sales revenue	1,380		1 Feb	Purchases		680
12 Feb	Cash		1,380	8 Feb	Non-current asset		900
25 Feb	SL control		700	12 Feb	Bank	1,380	
26 Feb	Sales revenue	1,560		22 Feb	PL control		600
26 Feb	Cash		1,560	26 Feb	Bank	1,560	
				26 Feb	Drawings		1,200

Task 5

Enter the following transactions for a business in the blank ledger accounts given below. Today's date is 4 March.

(a) Sale of goods on credit for £2,400
(b) Purchase of goods on credit for £1,800
(c) Payment of phone bill by cheque £140
(d) Withdrawal of cash from the bank account by the owner £500

Sales ledger control account

Date	Details	Amount £	Date	Details	Amount £

Sales revenue

Date	Details	Amount £	Date	Details	Amount £

Purchases

Date	Details	Amount £	Date	Details	Amount £

Purchases ledger control account

Date	Details	Amount £	Date	Details	Amount £

Phone

Date	Details	Amount £	Date	Details	Amount £

Bank/cash

Date	Details	Cash £	Bank £	Date	Details	Cash £	Bank £

Drawings

Date	Details	Amount £	Date	Details	Amount £

BALANCING AND CLOSING OFF THE LEDGER ACCOUNTS

Now that we have entered all of the transactions for the month in Jenny Fisher's ledger accounts the next stage is to find the closing balance on each account.

HOW IT WORKS

The steps to follow in finding the closing balance on a ledger account will be illustrated using Jenny Fisher's bank/cash account at the end of February.

Step 1 Total each column on both sides of the account making a working note of each total (£6,980 and £15,640 for the bank columns, £2,940 for each cash column). For the bank account, take the larger total and put this in as the total on both sides of the account leaving a spare line at the bottom of each side.

Bank/cash account

Date	Details	Cash £	Bank £	Date	Details	Cash £	Bank £
1 Feb	Capital		12,000	1 Feb	Rent		3,600
12 Feb	Sales revenue	1,380		1 Feb	Purchases		680
12 Feb	Cash		1,380	8 Feb	Non-current asset		900
25 Feb	SL control		700	12 Feb	Bank	1,380	
26 Feb	Sales revenue	1,560		22 Feb	PL control		600
26 Feb	Cash		1,560	26 Feb	Bank	1,560	
				26 Feb	Drawings		1,200
							6,980
		2,940	15,640			2,940	15,640

Step 2 Make the smaller of the two sides of the account add up to this total by putting in the balancing figure and describing it as the balance carried down (bal c/d) at the end of the month, 28 February. Show the same figure below the total on the other side of the account described as the balance brought down (bal b/d) at 1 March (the start of the new accounting period).

Bank/cash account

Date	Details	Cash £	Bank £	Date	Details	Cash £	Bank £
1 Feb	Capital		12,000	1 Feb	Rent		3,600
12 Feb	Sales revenue	1,380		1 Feb	Purchases		680
12 Feb	Cash		1,380	8 Feb	Non-current asset		900
25 Feb	SL control		700	12 Feb	Bank	1,380	
26 Feb	Sales revenue	1,560		22 Feb	PL control		600
26 Feb	Cash		1,560	26 Feb	Bank	1,560	
				26 Feb	Drawings		1,200
				28 Feb	Bal c/d		8,660
		2,940	15,640			2,940	15,640
1 Mar	Bal b/d		8,660				

This shows that Jenny has a balance of £8,660 in the bank account at the start of March. She had banked all her cash so she had no balance on the cash account.

Task 6

As at the end of February calculate and write in a balance carried down and a balance brought down on the following ledger account, including dates.

Sales ledger control account

Date	Details	Amount £	Date	Details	Amount £
17 Feb	Sales revenue	900	25 Feb	Bank/cash	700

PREPARING A TRIAL BALANCE

A TRIAL BALANCE is simply a list of all of the balances on the main ledger accounts split between the debit balances brought down and the credit balances brought down. One of the purposes of a trial balance is to serve as a check on the double entry bookkeeping. The total of the debit balances should be equal to the total of the credit balances and if there is an imbalance then this must be investigated and the cause of the imbalance corrected.

At this stage we are simply going to prepare the trial balance – dealing with imbalances and errors will be covered in Chapter 11.

HOW IT WORKS

Given below are all of the balanced ledger accounts for Jenny Fisher's first month of trading.

Bank/cash account

Date	Details	Cash £	Bank £	Date	Details	Cash £	Bank £
1 Feb	Capital		12,000	1 Feb	Rent		3,600
12 Feb	Sales revenue	1,380		1 Feb	Purchases		680
12 Feb	Cash		1,380	8 Feb	Non–current asset		900
25 Feb	SL control		700	12 Feb	Bank	1,380	
26 Feb	Sales revenue	1,560		22 Feb	PL control		600
26 Feb	Cash		1,560	26 Feb	Bank	1,560	
				26 Feb	Drawings		1,200
		____	____	28 Feb	Bal c/d	____	8,660
		2,940	15,640			2,940	15,640
1 Mar	Bal b/d		8,660				

Capital account

Date	Details	£	Date	Details	£
			1 Feb	Bank/cash	12,000

Rent account

Date	Details	£	Date	Details	£
1 Feb	Bank/cash	3,600			

Non-current asset account – computer

Date	Details	£	Date	Details	£
8 Feb	Bank/cash	900			

Purchases account

Date	Details	£	Date	Details	£
1 Feb	Bank/cash	680	28 Feb	Balance c/d	1,680
8 Feb	PL control	1,000			
		1,680			1,680
1 Mar	Balance b/d	1,680			

Purchases ledger control account

Date	Details	£	Date	Details	£
22 Feb	Bank/cash	600	8 Feb	Purchases	1,000
28 Feb	Balance c/d	400			
		1,000			1,000
			1 Mar	Balance b/d	400

Sales ledger control account

Date	Details	£	Date	Details	£
17 Feb	Sales revenue	900	25 Feb	Bank/cash	700
			28 Feb	Balance c/d	200
		900			900
1 Mar	Balance b/d	200			

Sales revenue account

Date	Details	£	Date	Details	£
28 Feb	Balance c/d	3,840	12 Feb	Bank/cash	1,380
			17 Feb	SL control	900
			26 Feb	Bank/cash	1,560
		3,840			3,840
			1 Mar	Balance b/d	3,840

Drawings account

Date	Details	£	Date	Details	£
26 Feb	Bank/cash	1,200			

The trial balance as at 28 February is drawn up by listing all of the balances b/d as either debit or credit balances.

Trial balance as at 28 February

	Debit £	Credit £
Bank/cash	8,660	
Capital		12,000
Rent	3,600	
Non-current asset – computer	900	
Purchases	1,680	
Payables		400
Receivables	200	
Sales revenue		3,840
Drawings	1,200	
	16,240	16,240

Note that the figure for payables is the balance on the purchases ledger control account and the figure for receivables is the balance on the sales ledger control account.

The total of the debit balances is equal to the total of the credit balances so the trial balance balances. This will not always be the case if errors have been made (see Chapter 11).

The closing balances at the end of February on these ledger accounts will still be the opening balances at the start of the next month's trading. Extracting a trial balance does not necessarily mean closing down a set of accounts.

BOOKS OF PRIME ENTRY AND DOUBLE ENTRY BOOKKEEPING

Above we took each of Jenny's transactions as it occurred and entered it into the ledger accounts as a debit and a credit. In practice this would be too time-consuming and therefore all similar transactions are gathered together into the books of prime entry and it is the totals of these that are regularly posted to the ledger accounts.

Task 7

What is a trial balance?

A   A list of ledger balances extracted from accounts which can act as a statement of financial position for a business.

B   A list of ledger balances extracted from accounts which helps to ensure that the bookkeeping has been accurate.

C   An accounting document which a business must prepare.

D   A list of all transactions which have occurred in a period taken from ledger accounts.

CHAPTER OVERVIEW

- The aim of any accounting system is to ensure that all transactions are accurately recorded in the financial records

- Each type of transaction that a business makes will be supported and evidenced by a primary record

- The main primary records for most businesses are receipts issued or till rolls, sales invoices and credit notes issued, cheques and remittance advice notes received from customers, purchase invoices and credit notes received, cheque book stubs for all types of payments, automated payment authorisations and petty cash vouchers

- Each type of primary record is recorded in its own book of prime entry

- Sales invoices are recorded in the sales day book and credit notes issued in the sales returns day book

- Purchase invoices are recorded in the purchases day book and credit notes received in the purchases returns day book

- Cheque and cash receipts, cheque payments and automated payments, and discounts received and allowed are all recorded in the three column cash book (often split into the cash receipts book and cash payments book)

- Petty cash payments are recorded in the petty cash book

- Non-standard transactions and payroll transactions are recorded in the journal

- The totals and details from the books of prime entry are recorded in the ledger accounts

- The principal ledgers are the general ledger and the memorandum ledgers, the sales ledger and the purchases ledger

- The cash book and the petty cash book usually operate as both books of prime entry and part of the general ledger

- The three principles of double entry bookkeeping are:
    - The dual effect of transactions
    - The separate entity concept
    - The accounting equation: assets minus liabilities equals capital

- The trial balance is a list of all of the balances in the general ledger – it is used in order to detect any errors in the ledger accounts and as a basis for preparing the financial statements

Keywords

Cash sales – sales that are made for immediate payment by cash, cheque, credit or debit card

Credit sales – sales that are made now but payment is not required for a specified period of time

Receivable – someone who owes money to the business (the balance on the sales ledger control account is usually taken as the trade receivables figure)

Sales returns – returns of goods from customers

Purchases – purchase either of materials that are to made into goods for resale or purchase of goods that are to be resold to customers

Cash purchases – purchases made where payment is required immediately

Credit purchases – purchases made now where payment is not required until the end of a specified period of time

Payable – someone who is owed money by the business (the balance on the purchases ledger control account is usually taken as the trade payables figure)

Purchases returns – returns of goods to suppliers

Capital expenditure – payments made for non-current assets

Non-current assets – assets that are to be used for the long term within the business

Revenue expenditure – payments for everyday business expenses other than the purchase of non-current assets

Primary document – the document that supports and evidences a business transaction

Primary record – the book of prime entry for recording the details about business transactions shown in the primary document

Sales invoice – issued by the seller to the purchaser of goods on credit showing the details of the goods sold, the amount due and the due date of payment

Credit note – a document issued to a customer who returns goods showing the details of the goods returned and their value

Remittance advice note – a document sent with a payment setting out which amounts are being paid, and whether any settlement discount is being taken

Cheque book stub – the part of a cheque that remains in the cheque book when the cheque is removed and sent out, recording the details of the cheque

Purchase invoice – an invoice received from a credit supplier detailing the goods purchased, the amount due and the due date of payment

Automated payments – payments made directly from one bank account to the bank account of another party such as standing orders, direct debits, bank giro credits and BACS payments

Petty cash box – the locked box in which any amounts of cash are kept on the business premises in order to make small cash payments

Petty cash voucher – the voucher that must be completed and authorised before any petty cash will be paid out

Book of prime entry – the initial record of each type of transaction – a list of each type of primary record

Sales day book – a list of each of the sales invoices sent out by the business to credit customers

Sales returns day book – a list of each of the credit notes issued by the business to credit customers

Purchases day book – a list of the invoices received from credit suppliers

Purchases returns day book – a list of the credit notes received from suppliers

Cash receipts book – a record of all of the cash and cheques received by the business

Cash payments book – a record of all of the cheques and any automated payments made

Petty cash book – details of all of the petty cash payments made and the receipt of cash into the petty cash box

Journal – the book of prime entry for non-standard transactions

General ledger – the ledger in which is kept a ledger account for each type of income, expense, asset and liability

Sales ledger control account – the account in the general ledger for receivables representing the total of amounts owed by trade receivables

Purchases ledger control account – the account in the general ledger for payables representing the total of amounts owed by all trade payables

Sales ledger – the ledger in which is kept an account for each individual receivable (customer)

Purchases ledger – the ledger in which is kept an account for each individual payable (supplier)

Accounting equation – ASSETS minus LIABILITIES equals CAPITAL

Trial balance – a list of the balances on each of the ledger accounts in the general ledger

TEST YOUR LEARNING

Test 1

Given below are the transactions of a new business for its first month. The business is not registered for VAT.

1 Mar	Owner pays £20,000 into a business bank account
1 Mar	Furniture and fittings purchased by cheque for the office premises £3,200
4 Mar	Purchases of goods for resale made by cheque for £4,400
6 Mar	Rent paid by cheque £600
10 Mar	Sales for £1,800 cheque received
15 Mar	Sales on credit £4,900
20 Mar	Purchases on credit £2,700
24 Mar	Cheque received from credit customers £3,500
28 Mar	Owner withdraws £1,000 in cash
29 Mar	Sales on credit £1,600
30 Mar	Cheque for £1,800 sent to credit supplier
31 Mar	Wages paid by cheque of £900

Write up each of these transactions in the ledger accounts of the business, balance any accounts with more than one entry and then prepare a trial balance as at 31 March.

Bank account

Date	Details	£	Date	Details	£

Capital account

Date	Details	£	Date	Details	£

Furniture and fittings account

Date	Details	£	Date	Details	£

Purchases account

Date	Details	£	Date	Details	£

Rent account

Date	Details	£	Date	Details	£

Sales revenue account

Date	Details	£	Date	Details	£

Sales ledger control account

Date	Details	£	Date	Details	£
		——			——
		══			══

Purchases ledger control account

Date	Details	£	Date	Details	£
		——			——
		══			══

Drawings account

Date	Details	£	Date	Details	£
		——			——
		══			══

Wages account

Date	Details	£	Date	Details	£
		——			——
		══			══

Trial balance as at 31 March

	Debit £	Credit £
Bank		
Capital		
Furniture and fittings		
Purchases		
Rent		
Sales revenue		
Receivables		
Payables		
Drawings		
Wages		

Test 2

Given below are the books of prime entry of a small business for its first month of trading. The business is not registered for VAT.

Sales day book

Date	Customer	Invoice No.	Total £
4 Mar	J Simpson	0001	420
12 Mar	F Barnet	0002	350
18 Mar	H Jerry	0003	180
28 Mar	D Dawson	0004	440
			1,390

Sales returns day book

Date	Customer	Credit note No.	Total £
19 Mar	F Barnet	CN 001	40
25 Mar	H Jerry	CN 002	20
			60

Purchases day book

Date	Customer	Invoice No.	Total £
1 Mar	L Lilley	89432	590
7 Mar	O Rools	12332	400
24 Mar	R Terry	0532	410
			1,400

Purchases returns day book

Date	Customer	Credit note No.	Total £
10 Mar	O Rools	C357	80

Cash receipts book

Date	Details	Total £	Cash sales £	Sales ledger £	Other £	Discounts allowed £
1 Mar	Capital	15,000			15,000	
7 Mar	Cash sales	930	930			
20 Mar	J Simpson	420		420		
22 Mar	Cash sales	740	740			
31 Mar	F Barnet	300		300		10
		17,390	1,670	720	15,000	10

Cash payments book

Date	Details	Cheque No.	Total £	Cash purchases £	Purchases ledger £	Wages £	Other £	Discounts received £
2 Mar	Cash purchases	0001	550	550				
6 Mar	Shop fittings	0002	1,100				1,100	
12 Mar	L Lilley	0003	560		560			30
15 Mar	Cash purchases	0004	780	780				
18 Mar	Cash purchases	0005	920	920				
20 Mar	O Rools	0006	310		310			10
31 Mar	Wages		2,200			2,200		
			6,420	2,250	870	2,200	1,100	40

You are required to:

(a) Post all of the books of prime entry to the relevant accounts in the general ledger

(b) Post the individual entries to the subsidiary ledgers, the sales ledger and the purchases ledger

(c) Balance all of the main ledger accounts and subsidiary ledger accounts

(d) Prepare a trial balance as at 31 March

General ledger

Sales ledger control account

Date	Details	£	Date	Details	£

Sales revenue account

Date	Details	£	Date	Details	£

Sales returns account

Date	Details	£	Date	Details	£

Purchases ledger control account

Date	Details	£	Date	Details	£

Purchases account

Date	Details	£	Date	Details	£

Purchases returns account

Date	Details	£	Date	Details	£

Capital account

Date	Details	£	Date	Details	£

Discounts allowed account

Date	Details	£	Date	Details	£

Wages account

Date	Details	£	Date	Details	£

Shop fittings account

Date	Details	£	Date	Details	£

Discounts received account

Date	Details	£	Date	Details	£

Bank/cash

Date	Details	£	Date	Details	£

Sales ledger

J Simpson

Date	Details	£	Date	Details	£

F Barnet

Date	Details	£	Date	Details	£

H Jerry

Date	Details	£	Date	Details	£

D Dawson

Date	Details	£	Date	Details	£

Purchases ledger

L Lilley

Date	Details	£	Date	Details	£

O Rools

Date	Details	£	Date	Details	£

R Terry

Date	Details	£	Date	Details	£

Trial balance as at 31 March

	Debit £	Credit £
Receivables		
Sales revenue		
Sales returns		
Payables		
Purchases		
Purchases returns		
Capital		
Discounts allowed		
Wages		
Shop fittings		
Discounts received		
Bank/cash		

chapter 2:
ACCOUNTING CONCEPTS

chapter coverage 📖

In this chapter we introduce the actual financial statements or final accounts that a business will eventually produce from the trial balance, namely the statement of profit or loss (income statement) and the statement of financial position. We also introduce some accounting concepts of which you need to be aware.

The topics covered are:

- ✍ The meaning of the balances in a trial balance
- ✍ The financial statements
- ✍ Preparing the financial statements from the ledger accounts
- ✍ Accounting standards
- ✍ Accounting principles and concepts
- ✍ Accounting characteristics

THE MEANING OF THE BALANCES IN A TRIAL BALANCE

Each balance in the trial balance will be one of the following:

- An asset
- A liability
- Income
- An expense
- Capital

You need to be able to distinguish between each of these types of balance.

HOW IT WORKS

Given below is the trial balance for Hunter Traders, a small business that is not registered for VAT. For each figure we have stated whether it is an asset, liability, income, expense or capital, with an explanation wherever necessary.

	Debit £	Credit £	Category
Non-current assets	10,200		asset
Bank	750		asset
Cash	50		asset
Heat and light	240		expense
Loan		2,000	liability
Capital		12,760	capital
Marketing	80		expense
Discounts received		280	income
Sales revenue		44,000	income
Opening inventory	2,400		(see note below)
Receivables	3,800		asset
Wages	10,400		expense
Discounts allowed	440		expense
Payables		2,400	liability
Rent	600		expense
Telephone	320		expense
Travel	160		expense
Drawings	4,000		(see note below)
Purchases	28,000		expense
	61,440	61,440	

INVENTORY items are goods which have been accounted for as purchases in the period in which they were first bought, but which have not been sold in that period. Consequently they are being held by the business until the following period. This means that at the end of the first period, and the beginning of the next period, inventory is an **asset**.

The inventory figure in any trial balance is always the amount brought forward from the previous period. This will be explained and expanded upon in Chapter 7.

Drawings – although a debit balance these are neither an expense nor an asset. Drawings are instead a reduction in **capital**.

Task 1

Given below is the trial balance of a small trader, N Lawson, who is not registered for VAT. In the space next to each balance you are required to state whether the balance is an asset, liability, income, expense or capital.

	£	Description
Rent	480	
Motor van	7,400	
Payables	1,900	
Heat and light	210	
Discounts received	50	
Motor expenses	310	
Sales revenue	40,800	
Opening inventory	2,100	
Loan	2,000	
Stationery	330	
Capital	7,980	
Phone	640	
Discount allowed	60	
Purchases	22,600	
Receivables	3,400	
Wages	9,700	

	£	Description
Drawings	4,000	
Office cleaning	220	
Travel and accommodation	660	
Bank	483	
Cash	137	

THE FINANCIAL STATEMENTS

The statement of profit or loss (SPL)

The STATEMENT OF PROFIT OR LOSS (known in UK GAAP accounting terminology as the PROFIT AND LOSS ACCOUNT) is a summary of the activity of the organisation during the year. It is, in simple terms, a statement of the following:

INCOME minus EXPENSES equals PROFIT OR LOSS

- If the **income is greater than** the expenses then a **profit** is made
- If the **expenses exceed the income** then a **loss** has been made

However despite the simple concept of the statement of profit or loss it is normally laid out in a particular manner. Prior to the most recent amendment to IAS 1, the statement of profit or loss was known as the income statement.

HOW IT WORKS

The trial balance for Hunter Traders and its statement of profit or loss are set out below, together with an explanation of the important points. You will see that each item denoted as income or expense from the trial balance is used in the statement of profit or loss. As you work through each figure in the statement of profit or loss, tick it off on the trial balance to show that all of the income and expenses are included.

Trial balance

	Debit £	Credit £	Category
Non-current assets	10,200		asset
Bank	750		asset
Cash	50		asset
Heat and light	240		expense
Loan		2,000	liability
Capital		12,760	capital
Marketing	80		expense
Discounts received		280	income
Sales revenue		44,000	income
Opening inventory	2,400		(see note below)
Receivables	3,800		asset
Wages	10,400		expense
Discounts allowed	440		expense
Payables		2,400	liability
Rent	600		expense
Telephone	320		expense
Travel	160		expense
Drawings	4,000		reduction in capital
Purchases	28,000		expense
	61,440	61,440	

In order to produce the statement of profit or loss there is one further figure that is required. This is the value of the closing inventory at the date of the trial balance, which for Hunter Traders is £3,200. We need this figure so that we can calculate the cost of the goods actually sold in the period. This will not necessarily be the actual purchases in the period because, as we saw earlier, some of the purchases in the period may still be in stock at the end of the period. In addition, the opening inventory will have been sold during the current period. The statement of profit or loss therefore needs to take into account both the 'using up' of the opening inventory balance and the retention of the closing inventory balance. Note where these figures are in the statement of profit or loss below: this will be covered in detail in Chapter 7.

Statement of profit or loss

	£	£
Sales revenue		44,000
Less cost of sales		
Opening inventory	2,400	
Purchases	28,000	
	30,400	
Less closing inventory	(3,200)	
Cost of sales		(27,200)
Gross profit		16,800
Discounts received		280
		17,080
Less expenses		
Heat and light	240	
Marketing	80	
Discounts allowed	440	
Wages	10,400	
Travel	160	
Rent	600	
Telephone	320	
		(12,240)
Profit for the year		4,840

Gross profit – the first part ends in GROSS PROFIT: the profit earned by the business's trading activities. As you can see it is calculated as the sales value less the cost of those sales. This area will be considered in more detail in Chapter 7.

Expenses – the second part consists of a list of all of the business's expenses.

Discounts – discounts allowed to customers are an expense of the business and are therefore included in the list of expenses. Discounts received however are similar to income as they are a benefit to the business. Discounts received are normally shown as income just below the gross profit line. They may also be shown as a negative expense item (in brackets to indicate that the amount is to be deducted from the expenses).

Profit for the year – the PROFIT FOR THE YEAR is the final profit of the business after all expenses have been deducted.

Task 2

A business has made sales of £136,700 and its purchases totalled £97,500. The opening inventory was £11,300 and the closing inventory was £10,600. What is the business's gross profit?

£ [   ]

The statement of financial position (SFP)

Whereas the statement of profit or loss is a history of the transactions of the business during the accounting period the STATEMENT OF FINANCIAL POSITION (or SFP) in contrast is simply a 'snap shot' of the business on the final day of the accounting period. In UK GAAP accounting terminology the statement of financial position is called the BALANCE SHEET.

The statement of financial position (SFP) is a list of all of the assets, liabilities and capital of the business. It is also an expression of the accounting equation. Remember that the accounting equation is:

ASSETS minus LIABILITIES equals CAPITAL

The SFP is a vertical form of the accounting equation. It lists and totals the assets of the business and deducts the liabilities. This total is then shown to be equal to the capital of the business, which has been increased by the period's profit or decreased by its loss.

HOW IT WORKS

When producing its statement of profit or loss, in Hunter Traders' trial balance we ticked off all the expenses and income. This left a number of un-ticked items which will now all appear in the statement of financial position.

Like the statement of profit or loss the statement of financial position is laid out in a particular format. The UK balance sheet format is illustrated below for Hunter Traders.

Statement of financial position

	£	£	£
Non-current assets			10,200
Current assets:			
Inventory	3,200		
Receivables	3,800		
Bank/cash	800		
		7,800	
Current liabilities:			
Payables		(2,400)	
Net current assets			5,400
			15,600
Non-current liabilities:			
Loan			(2,000)
Net assets			13,600

Financed by:

	£
Capital (at the start of the period)	12,760
Add profit for the period (from the statement of profit or loss)	4,840
	17,600
Less drawings in the period	(4,000)
	13,600

Accounting equation – the statement of financial position falls naturally into two parts which are the two sides of the accounting equation – 'assets minus liabilities' (often known as NET ASSETS) and 'capital'.

Non-current assets – non-current assets are always shown as the first assets on the statement of financial position as they are the major long-term assets of the business.

Current assets – the CURRENT ASSETS of a business are the other, shorter term, assets: inventory followed by receivables and the money held in the bank account as cash in hand and as petty cash. Note that as the statement of financial position is prepared on the final day of the accounting period it is the closing inventory figure which is included in the statement of financial position.

Current liabilities – the CURRENT LIABILITIES of a business are the short term payables.

Net current assets – the NET CURRENT ASSETS figure is a sub-total of the current assets less the current liabilities. The net current asset total is then added in to the non-current asset total.

Non-current liabilities – the NON-CURRENT LIABILITIES are liabilities that are due to be paid after more than one year. In this case we have assumed that the loan is a long term loan, ie, is repayable after more than one year.

Net assets – the total for non-current liabilities is deducted from the total of non-current assets and net current assets to give the STATEMENT OF FINANCIAL POSITION TOTAL. In terms of the accounting equation this is the total of the assets minus liabilities, also known as NET ASSETS.

Capital – the 'financed by' section of the statement of financial position shows the amounts that are owed back to the owner of the business, that is their total capital. This consists of the amount of the owner's capital at the start of the accounting period plus the profit that the business has earned (this figure of £4,840 is the net profit taken from the statement of profit or loss) less the drawings that the owner has taken out of the business during the accounting period. The total of the capital section is also the statement of financial position total ie it should equal the net assets total.

Note that drawings are part of the statement of financial position and are not included as expenses – they are a reduction of capital.

Task 3

Given below is the trial balance of N Lawson. In the space next to each balance state whether the balance would appear in the statement of profit or loss or in the statement of financial position.

	Debit	Credit	Statement of profit or loss (✓)	Statement of financial position (✓)
	£	£		
Rent	480			
Motor van	7,400			
Payables		1,900		
Heat and light	210			
Discounts received		50		
Motor expenses	310			
Sales revenue		40,800		
Opening inventory	2,100			
Loan		2,000		
Stationery	330			
Capital		7,980		
Phone	640			
Discount allowed	60			
Purchases	22,600			
Receivables	3,400			
Wages	9,700			
Drawings	4,000			
Office cleaning	220			
Travel and accommodation	660			
Bank	483			
Cash	137			
	52,730	52,730		

PREPARING THE FINANCIAL STATEMENTS FROM THE LEDGER ACCOUNTS

Before we leave the subject of the financial statements we must consider how the statement of profit or loss and the statement of financial position are prepared from the general ledger accounts.

There is a distinct difference between the statement of profit or loss ledger accounts and the statement of financial position ledger accounts.

- The STATEMENT OF PROFIT OR LOSS is effectively a large ledger account in its own right. This means that each of the balances on **income** and **expense** accounts are transferred or 'cleared' to the profit and loss ledger account at the end of the accounting period. The effect of this is that there is no opening balance on the income and expense ledger accounts at the start of the following accounting period

- In contrast the STATEMENT OF FINANCIAL POSITION is a list of all of the balances on the **asset**, **liability** and **capital** accounts (the drawings account is cleared to the capital account at the end of each period, along with the balance on the statement of profit or loss itself). These assets, liabilities and capital will still exist at the start of the next accounting period and so the balances on these accounts are simply listed in the statement of financial position. They are carried down in the ledger accounts as the brought down or opening balances at the start of the next accounting period

ACCOUNTING STANDARDS

The way in which some entities, notably companies, prepare their annual financial statements is regulated both by the law and the accounting profession. The purpose of this regulation is to try to ensure that the financial statements of different companies and different types of business are as comparable as possible.

Many small businesses do not operate as companies and so the law in this area (the Companies Act 2006) does not affect them.

They are more affected by the accounting profession which aims to prepare financial statements for businesses in accordance with accounting standards that the profession issues. The aims of accounting standards are to:

- Reduce the variety of methods of dealing with accounting issues

- Set out the best method to use in order to increase the comparability of the financial statements of different organisations

UK accounting standards are either Statements of Standard Accounting Practice (SSAPs) or Financial Reporting Standards (FRSs). Together with UK company law, these rules are often referred to as 'UK GAAP' – or UK Generally Accepted Accounting Practice.

Accounting practice in the UK and elsewhere is increasingly influenced by International Accounting Standards (IASs) and International Financial Reporting Standards (IFRSs), issued by the International Accounting Standards Board (IASB). Many IASs and IFRSs take the same, or very similar, approaches to accounting as the UK SSAPs and FRSs.

There are some important differences in terminology between UK GAAP and IASs:

IASs/IFRSs	UK GAAP
Non-current assets	Fixed assets
Inventory	Stock
Receivable	Debtor
Payable	Creditor
Irrecoverable debt	Bad debt
Statement of profit or loss (SPL)	Profit and loss account (P&L)
Statement of financial position (SFP)	Balance sheet (BS)

In this Text we use the IFRS terms; AAT assessments from 1 January 2012 use IFRS terminology.

For the purposes of Accounts Preparation the following accounting standards will be covered:

- Non-current assets – the international IAS 16 (Property, plant and equipment) in Chapters 3, 4 and 5

- Inventory – the international IAS 2 (Inventories) in Chapter 7

ACCOUNTING PRINCIPLES AND CONCEPTS

A business's final ledger accounts and financial statements are prepared according to well-known and well-understood ACCOUNTING CONCEPTS.

Two fundamental concepts – the GOING CONCERN CONCEPT and the ACCRUALS CONCEPT – play a very pervasive role in the preparation of financial statements. In addition the PRUDENCE CONCEPT and the CONSISTENCY CONCEPT must be applied to the production of accounting information.

Going concern concept

The going concern concept is that a business will continue for the foreseeable future.

This concept affects in particular the values of non-current assets shown in the statement of financial position.

- If the business is a going concern then non-current assets will be shown in the statement of financial position at the amount that they cost less accumulated depreciation (we shall see what this means in Chapter 4)

- If the business is not a going concern and instead is due to close down in the near future then its non-current assets (such as specialised premises or machinery) have a very low value because they probably cannot easily be sold when the business closes. This value may be less than the amount that the assets cost in the first place, so the amount at which they are shown in the statement of financial position will be different than if the business was a going concern

Accruals concept

The accruals concept is that the effects of transactions are reflected in the financial statements for the period in which they occur rather than in the period in which any cash involved is received or paid.

This means that the amount of any income or expense appearing in the statement of profit or loss should be the amount that was earned or incurred during the accounting period rather than the amount of cash that was received or paid.

We have already come across examples of this with credit sales and credit purchases. When a sale is made on credit, the sales account is credited immediately even though it may be a number of weeks before the cash is actually received from the customer.

We will come across further examples of applying the accruals concept when we deal with depreciation in Chapter 4 and accruals and prepayments in Chapter 6.

Prudence

Where there are conditions of uncertainty, amounts in financial statements need to be treated with PRUDENCE. This means that a degree of caution is required so that assets or income are not overstated and liabilities or expenses are not understated.

Prudence must be exercised when preparing financial statements because of the uncertainty that surrounds many transactions, such as whether debts from credit

customers will be paid, and how long plant and machinery will be usable in the business.

Exercising prudence generally means that the **most cautious amount for assets is included in financial statements**. For example, in theory a business could choose to value its inventory at its selling price, but prudence tells us that this price may not be achieved, so the more cautious option of using its purchase price is chosen instead.

In addition, if a business **foresees a loss** but the exact amount of the loss is not known, an estimate should be made with a degree of caution, based on the best information available. For example, if a business purchases inventory for £1,200 but, because of a sudden slump in the market, only £900 is likely to be realised when the inventory is sold, the cautious valuation is that the inventory is valued at £900.

Consistency

To make financial statements more useful and comparable the CONSISTENCY CONCEPT is applied. This means that the presentation and classification of items in the financial statements should stay the same from one period to the next, unless there is a very good reason to change. Thus if a business treats capital expenditure of £500 or more as a non-current asset in its statement of financial position in one year, it should apply the same policy in the following year rather than deciding to treat capital expenditure on items of £100 or more as a non-current asset.

Task 4

Credit sales and credit purchases are recorded in the books of account as they take place rather than when cash is received or paid. This demonstrates which accounting concept?

Going concern/accruals/prudence/consistency

ACCOUNTING CHARACTERISTICS

The qualitative characteristics of financial information are those attributes that make the information useful to users. The *Conceptual Framework for Financial Reporting* issued by the IASB identifies two fundamental qualitative characteristics (relevance and faithful representation) and four enhancing qualitative characteristics (comparability, verifiability, timeliness and understandability).

The *Conceptual Framework* also identifies the characteristic of materiality that underpins the fundamental characteristic of relevance.

We will consider first the two fundamental qualitative characteristics of relevance, together with materiality, and faithful representation.

Relevance

Information has the quality of RELEVANCE when it influences the economic decisions of users by helping them evaluate past, present or future events. Financial information may confirm past events or may provide the basis for predicting future events.

Materiality

Information is material if its omission or misstatement could influence the decisions made by users of that information. MATERIALITY is an entity-specific aspect of relevance.

Materiality concerns the accounting treatment of 'small' or non-material items in the financial statements. What it means in practical terms is that although there are certain rules which underlie the preparation of financial statements these rules do not necessarily need to apply to non-material items.

For example, we have seen that assets that are for long-term use in the business should be shown as non-current assets in the statement of financial position. However, small items such as calculators and staplers for use in the office need not be treated as non-current assets if it is decided that they are not material – instead their cost would simply be an expense in the statement of profit or loss. Similarly office stationery that is used in the business will be charged as an expense in the statement of profit or loss. This expense should strictly be adjusted to reflect any inventory of stationery left at the end of the year. However if these amounts are deemed to be immaterial then no adjustment is required.

What is a material amount? The answer to this will depend upon the size of the business itself. In some large businesses the materiality level may be set at something like £5,000. However, in a small business it would be much lower, maybe with balances of £100 or less being considered immaterial.

Faithful representation

Financial information should be complete, neutral and free from error. Although the *Conceptual Framework* recognises that perfection is not always possible, financial information should faithfully represent what it purports to represent. This means including all relevant information without bias and with a high degree of accuracy.

We will now consider the four enhancing qualitative characteristics of comparability, verifiability, timeliness and understandability.

Comparability

COMPARABILITY requires consistency of treatment so that users can compare financial statements over time, to identify trends, and with the financial statements of other businesses, to evaluate their relative position and performance.

Verifiability

VERIFIABILITY in financial information is achieved when it is free from material error and bias and can be depended on by users to be a faithful representation of what it is intended to represent.

Timeliness

TIMELINESS means that financial information should be made available to users without undue delay. Generally speaking up-to-date information is more useful than older information, although historical information can be useful in identifying trends.

Understandability

UNDERSTANDABILITY is essential if users are to make the most of financial statements. Users are assumed to have some business, economic and accounting knowledge and to be able to study the information properly.

CHAPTER OVERVIEW

- The statement of profit or loss shows the income of the business minus the expenses which will then give either a profit or a loss

- The statement of profit or loss is a historical summary of the activities of the business during the accounting period

- The gross profit is the profit made from the trading activities of the business. Once all of the expenses have been deducted then there will be a profit or loss for the year

- Discounts allowed are expenses however discounts received can either be shown as income just below gross profit or as a negative expense, ie, as a reduction of the expenses total

- The statement of financial position is a 'snap-shot' of the business on the last day of the accounting period listing all of the assets and liabilities of the business (its net assets)

- The statement of financial position is a vertical form of the accounting equation showing that the net assets equal the capital balance

- The assets are listed in a particular order starting with non-current (fixed) assets and followed by current assets. The current assets are listed in a particular order starting with inventory and working down to bank and cash balances

- Current liabilities are the payables of the business that are due to be paid in less than 12 months' time – current liabilities are deducted from the total of the current assets to give a figure known as the net current assets

- Non-current liabilities payable after more than 12 months are deducted from the total of net current assets and non-current assets to give the final statement of financial position total for net assets

- Capital is made up of the opening balance of capital plus the profit/minus the loss for the year from the statement of profit or loss minus the owner's drawings, coming to the same statement of financial position total as that for net assets

- The statement of profit or loss is a large, summary ledger account to which income and expense ledger accounts are cleared at the end of the accounting period leaving no remaining balances on these accounts

- In contrast the statement of financial position is a list of the asset, liability and capital account balances on the last day of the accounting period – these balances remain in the ledger accounts to become the opening balances at the start of the next accounting period

BPP
LEARNING MEDIA

- The format of a business's accounts is regulated by law (companies only) and accounting standards

- A business is a going concern, and the going concern concept should be applied to its accounts, if it will continue for the foreseeable future

- The accrual basis of preparing final accounts is that income and expenses should be included in the final accounts in the period in which they are earned or incurred rather than in the period in which the cash is received or paid

- The concept of prudence must be applied in preparing accounts so that assets and income are not overstated and liabilities and expenses are not understated

- The consistency concept is applied to accounts to ensure they are useful and comparable

- Financial information should have the fundamental qualitative characteristics of relevance and faithful representation, and the enhancing qualitative characteristics of comparability, verifiability, timeliness and understandability

- Materiality is an aspect of relevance that is entity-specific. It allows immaterial items to be treated in a manner which would not be appropriate for material items – the level of materiality will depend upon the size of the business

Keywords

Statement of profit or loss (SPL) – one of the main financial statements showing the income of the business less the expenses of the business for the last accounting period

Profit and loss account – the UK GAAP accounting term for the statement of profit or loss

Gross profit – the profit earned by the business from its trading activities (sales less cost of sales)

Profit for the year – the final profit of the business after all expenses have been deducted

Statement of financial position (SFP) – a list of all of the assets and liabilities of the business on the last day of the accounting period

Balance sheet – the UK GAAP accounting term for the statement of financial position

Current assets – the short term assets of the business – inventory, receivables and cash and bank balances

Current liabilities – liabilities that are due to be paid within one year of the statement of financial position (SFP) date

Net current assets – the total of the current assets minus the current liabilities

Non-current liabilities – liabilities that are due to be paid more than a year after the statement of financial position (SFP) date

Net assets – total assets less total liabilities as shown in the top half of the statement of financial position (SFP)

SSAPs – Statements of Standard Accounting Practice

FRSs – Financial Reporting Standards

IASs – International Accounting Standards

IFRSs – International Financial Reporting Standards

Going concern concept – financial statements are prepared on the basis that the organisation will continue in business for the foreseeable future

Accruals concept – income and expenses are recognised in the period in which they were earned or incurred rather than when the cash was received or paid

Prudence concept – caution is required in preparing accounts to ensure that assets and income are not overstated and liabilities and expenses are not understated

Consistency concept – a business should apply policies consistently when preparing accounts so the results are comparable across time and with those of other businesses

Fundamental qualitative characteristics – relevance and faithful representation

Enhancing qualitative characteristics – comparability, verifiability, timeliness and understandability

Materiality – the rules of accounting do not need to be applied to immaterial items

TEST YOUR LEARNING

Test 1

Given below is the trial balance for a small business that is not registered for VAT. You are required to state, in the space next to each balance, whether it is an asset, liability, income, expense or capital and whether the balance would appear in the statement of profit or loss (SPL) or the statement of financial position (SFP).

	Debit £	Credit £	Type of balance	SPL or SFP
Sales revenue		41,200		
Loan		1,500		
Wages	7,000			
Non-current assets	7,100			
Opening inventory	1,800			
Receivables	3,400			
Discounts received		40		
Postage	100			
Bank	300			
Capital		9,530		
Rent	500			
Purchases	30,100			
Payables		2,500		
Discounts allowed	70			
Drawings	3,000			
Electricity	800			
Telephone	600			
	54,770	54,770		

Test 2

Complete the following sentences:

(a) The gross profit of a business is the profit from _____.

(b) The total of the current assets minus the current liabilities is known as _____.

Test 3

Each of the following statements is an example of which accounting concept?

(a) Sales on credit are recognised as sales at the date that the sales invoice is sent out to the customer. [ ]

(b) Non-current assets are valued in the statement of financial position at an amount based on their original cost to the business. [ ] [ ]

(c) Staplers for the office have been charged as an expense to the statement of profit or loss. [ ]

chapter 3:
PURCHASE OF NON-CURRENT ASSETS

chapter coverage 📖

In this chapter we start to consider the first unit of Accounts Preparation, 'Accounting for non-current assets'. We consider the distinction between capital expenditure and revenue expenditure and how to account for and control non-current assets.

The topics covered are:

✍ Capital and revenue expenditure

✍ Accounting for non-current asset acquisitions

✍ Authorisation for non-current asset acquisition

✍ Methods of funding

✍ Recording acquisitions in the non-current asset register

CAPITAL AND REVENUE EXPENDITURE

Some of the items that a business spends its money on will be fairly major long-term assets of the business, some will be assets that are due to be sold shortly and some will be the business's everyday running expenses.

Non-current assets

The assets that are purchased by a business for long-term use in the business are known as NON-CURRENT ASSETS. Non-current assets are necessary for the business to carry on its activities over more than one accounting period. Typical examples include:

- Buildings from which the business operates (classed as land and buildings)

- Machinery used in the manufacturing process (classed as machinery)

- Delivery vehicles to distribute goods (classed as motor vehicles)

- Cars for managers and sales representatives (classed as motor vehicles)

- Furniture and fittings for the office area (classed as furniture and fittings)

- Computers for the sales and administration departments (classed as computer equipment)

The cost of buying these non-current assets and getting them into operation is known as CAPITAL EXPENDITURE.

All other expenditure of the business, other than on the purchase of non-current assets, is known as REVENUE EXPENDITURE.

The distinction between capital and revenue expenditure

The importance of the distinction between revenue and capital expenditure is due to their differing treatment in the financial statements.

Capital expenditure is classified as a non-current asset and as such is included as an asset in the statement of financial position. Revenue expenditure, in contrast, is charged as an expense to the statement of profit or loss.

HOW IT WORKS

A business spends £20,000 on a new machine to be used for making its products. If this were mistakenly classified as revenue expenditure then the statement of profit or loss would have an extra large expense of £20,000 and the statement of financial position would not include this major asset of the business.

What is included in capital expenditure?

Due to the differing treatment of capital and revenue expenditure we must ensure that the correct amounts are included in the statement of financial position as capital expenditure.

The cost of a non-current asset to be included in the statement of financial position, or CAPITALISED, is not just its purchase price. It is the directly attributable costs of getting the asset to its correct location and into full working order. Therefore the costs that might be included as capital expenditure include:

- The purchase price (acquisition cost) of the asset net of VAT (although on cars that have some private use the VAT is irrecoverable and must be included in the purchase price)
- Delivery/handling costs
- Site preparation, installation, assembly and set-up costs
- Testing costs to ensure the asset is functioning properly
- Any special alterations or equipment required in order to use the asset
- Professional fees such as legal fees

IAS 16 (Property, plant and equipment) makes it clear that any major alteration or improvement of the asset is to be treated as capital expenditure.

Revenue expenditure

There will often be other expenses related to the non-current assets of a business and care must be taken to ensure that these are not capitalised in the statement of financial position but are treated as revenue expenditure and charged as expenses in the statement of profit or loss.

Examples of revenue expenditure which might be confused with capital expenditure include:

- Costs of decorating a new building
- Repairs to a building or machinery
- General maintenance costs
- Costs of cleaning machinery

- Fuel costs
- Administrative and general overheads such as insurance costs
- Servicing and repairs to motor vehicles
- The road fund licence for a vehicle (often included in the invoice for a new vehicle, so take care)
- CDs and printer paper for a computer

Capitalisation policy

Not all items that could be classified as capital expenditure have to be capitalised. A business may decide that non-material items purchased for long-term use in the business are too small in amount to be capitalised. For instance, the CAPITALISATION POLICY may be that a separate amount of expenditure on any item costing less than £100 – on a stapler for office use, say, or a toolbox for use in a workshop – should be treated as revenue rather than capital expenditure.

In addition, the business may decide to exclude from its capitalisation policy any assets that have a short expected LIFESPAN in use in the business. For instance, a PC could be used for many years in some businesses but may have only a short expected lifespan in a business where it would be used very heavily. Such a business's capitalisation policy would therefore state that assets with a restricted lifespan should be treated as revenue expenditure.

Assets made by the business's employees

In some situations non-current assets may not be purchased but are instead made or constructed by the business's employees. For example, a building firm may build a new set of offices for its own use.

Another situation might be that a business uses its own employees to install a new piece of machinery.

In each case the cost of the non-current asset will include the wages cost of the employees who worked on it together with the cost of any materials that they used. Therefore these wages and materials will be treated as capital expenditure.

HOW IT WORKS

Harris Incorporated have just significantly enlarged the operations of their manufacturing business and as such have purchased a number of major assets.

Purchased a building to use as the factory at a cost of £80,000 plus £1,000 of legal fees

- The legal fees are part of the cost of purchasing the building and therefore are treated as capital expenditure – total capital expenditure £81,000

Carried out £10,000 of building work in order to make the building suitable for the manufacturing process

- Again this is part of the cost of the factory and would be treated as capital expenditure of £10,000

Purchased a TV1 machine for £4,000 which was installed by Harris's own employees using £200 of materials and incurring wages costs of £600

- The installation costs should be treated as capital expenditure as they are a cost of getting the asset into use – total capital expenditure £4,800

Redecorated a building that was already owned and is used for the sales and administration departments at a total cost of £1,400

- This is all revenue expenditure as these are running expenses of the business – total revenue expenditure £1,400

Purchased a computer to help in the administration department for £1,200 together with computer software costing £400 and a training course for the employees who will be using the computer at a cost of £200. The cost of the computer included £50 of CDs and £20 of printer paper that were delivered with it

- The cost of the software could be treated as either capital or revenue expenditure – as the cost of this software is quite large it would probably be treated as capital expenditure. The cost of the training course would also be treated as capital expenditure as it is necessary in order to run the computer. The cost of the CDs and the paper is revenue expenditure as this is part of the cost of running the computer – total capital expenditure of £1,730, total revenue expenditure £70

Employed contract cleaners to clean the new TV1 machine after its first week of operation at a cost of £150

- This would be treated as revenue expenditure as it is part of the general running costs of the business – total revenue expenditure £150

Purchased a new delivery van at a cost of £16,400 which included £100 of delivery charges and £200 of road fund licence

- The delivery charges are part of the cost of the non-current (non-current) asset and are treated as capital expenditure but the road fund licence is a running cost of the vehicle and is treated as revenue expenditure – total capital expenditure £16,200, total revenue expenditure £200

Purchased some office furniture for £1,300 on credit

- Total capital expenditure £1,300

Purchased a car for £15,000, paying £10,000 cash and receiving a part exchange allowance of £5,000 on an old car which it traded in

- Irrespective of how the acquisition was funded, the total capital expenditure is £15,000

Task 1

A business has two machines. Machine A has just undergone a major overhaul at a cost of £15,000 which has extended its life to the business by four years. Machine B has just been repaired due to the wearing out of a small working part at a cost of £4,000. Identify the capital and the revenue expenditure incurred.

Capital expenditure £ [   ]

Revenue expenditure £ [   ]

ACCOUNTING FOR NON-CURRENT ASSET ACQUISITIONS

When non-current assets are purchased they are debited to separate asset ledger accounts for each type of non-current asset. The most common classifications of types of non-current asset are:

- Land and buildings
- Machinery
- Motor vehicles
- Furniture and fittings
- Computers

The assets may be purchased:

- For cash (ie by cheque), so the credit entry will be to the bank/cash account

- On credit, so the credit entry will be to the purchases ledger control account for a purchase on credit

- By means of a part exchange (or trade in) of an old asset. The value given in part exchange is debited to the non-current asset account, and the credit goes to the disposal account – we shall come back to the reasons for this in Chapter 5

- With a loan

- With a hire purchase or finance lease arrangement

When the business's own employees have made or installed non-current assets then the following double entry must be made:

Materials	Debit Non-current asset account
	Credit Purchases account
Wages	Debit Non-current asset account
	Credit Wages account

The effect of this is to remove the materials and wages that are capital expenditure from revenue expenditure accounts.

HOW IT WORKS

We will now return to Harris Incorporated and show how each item of expenditure would be entered into the ledger accounts. All of the purchases were for cash other than the office furniture which was purchased on credit, and the car which was paid for partly in cash and partly by part exchanging an old vehicle.

Purchased a building to use as the factory at a cost of £80,000 plus £1,000 of legal fees

Land and buildings account GL001

	£		£
Bank/cash	81,000		

Bank/cash account GL002

	£		£
		Land and buildings	81,000

Carried out £10,000 of building work in order to make the building suitable for the manufacturing process

Land and buildings account GL001

	£		£
Bank/cash	81,000		
Bank/cash	10,000		

Bank/cash account GL002

	£		£
		Land and buildings	81,000
		Land and buildings	10,000

Purchased a TV1 machine for £4,000 which was installed by Harris's own employees using £200 of materials and incurring wages costs of £600

Machinery account GL003

	£		£
Bank/cash	4,000		
Purchases	200		
Wages	600		

Bank/cash account GL002

	£		£
		Land and buildings	81,000
		Land and buildings	10,000
		Machinery	4,000

Purchases account GL100

	£		£
		Machinery	200

Wages account GL200

	£		£
		Machinery	600

Redecorated a building that was already owned and is used for the sales and administration departments at a total cost of £1,400

Buildings maintenance account GL110

	£		£
Bank/cash	1,400		

This is an expense account not a non-current asset account as this is revenue expenditure.

Bank/cash account GL002

	£		£
		Land and buildings	81,000
		Land and buildings	10,000
		Machinery	4,000
		Buildings maintenance	1,400

Purchased a computer to help in the administration department for £1,200 together with computer software costing £400. The cost of the computer included £50 of CDs and £20 of printer paper that were delivered with it

Computers account GL004

	£		£
Bank/cash	1,530		

Stationery account GL120

	£		£
Bank/cash	70		

The CDs and the paper have been charged to an expense account as they are revenue expenditure not capital expenditure.

Bank/cash account GL002

	£		£
		Land and buildings	81,000
		Land and buildings	10,000
		Machinery	4,000
		Buildings maintenance	1,400
		Computers	1,530
		Stationery	70

Employed contract cleaners to clean the new TV1 machine after its first week of operation at a cost of £150

Cleaning costs account GL130

	£		£
Bank/cash	150		

This is an expense account as this is revenue expenditure not capital expenditure.

Bank/cash account GL002

£		£
	Land and buildings	81,000
	Land and buildings	10,000
	Machinery	4,000
	Buildings maintenance	1,400
	Computers	1,530
	Stationery	70
	Cleaning costs	150

Purchased a new delivery van at a cost of £16,400 which included £100 of delivery charges and £200 of road fund licence

Motor vehicles account GL005

	£		£
Bank/cash	16,200		

Motor expenses GL140

	£		£
Bank/cash	200		

Again this is an expense account as the road fund licence is not capital expenditure.

Bank/cash account GL002

£		£
	Land and buildings	81,000
	Land and buildings	10,000
	Machinery	4,000
	Buildings maintenance	1,400
	Computers	1,530
	Stationery	70
	Cleaning costs	150
	Motor vehicles	16,200
	Motor expenses	200

Purchased some office furniture for £1,300 on credit

Furniture and fittings account GL006

	£		£
Purchases ledger control	1,300		

Purchases ledger control account GL007

	£		£
		Furniture and fittings	1,300

Purchased a car for £15,000, paying £10,000 cash and receiving a part exchange allowance of £5,000 on an old car which it traded in

Motor vehicles account GL005

	£		£
Bank/cash	16,200		
Bank/cash	10,000		
Disposal	5,000		

Bank/cash account GL002

	£		£
		Land and buildings	81,000
		Land and buildings	10,000
		Machinery	4,000
		Buildings maintenance	1,400
		Computers	1,530
		Stationery	70
		Cleaning costs	150
		Motor vehicles	16,200
		Motor expenses	200
		Motor vehicles	10,000

Disposal GL008

	£		£
		Motor vehicles	5,000

At the end of each accounting period, the balance on each non-current asset account will be carried down as the opening balance in the new period's accounts. Each carried down balance will also appear on the statement of financial position at the end of the old accounting period.

Task 2

A business has recently installed a new machine which cost £17,000 and was purchased on credit. The installation was carried out by its own employees and the wages costs of these employees for the time taken to install the machine are £1,400.

Write up the relevant ledger accounts to reflect the purchase and installation of this machine.

Machinery account

	£		£

Purchases ledger control account

	£		£

Wages account

	£		£

Journal entries

In practice the way in which the acquisition of a non-current asset is recorded in the ledger accounts is usually by way of a journal entry if it is acquired on credit or using part-exchange. If the asset is acquired for cash then the cash payments book is the book of prime entry for non-current assets.

In order to demonstrate clearly the double entry required in respect of non-current assets we shall produce journal entries for each of them.

HOW IT WORKS

Returning to Harris Incorporated we will now prepare the journal entries for each of the purchases of non-current assets (in practice of course this would be done before the entries are made in the ledger accounts as the journal is the instruction to make the ledger account entries). Today's date is 5 February 20XX.

Purchased a building to use as the factory at a cost of £80,000 plus £1,000 of legal fees, paid in cash

Date	Account	Ref	Debit £	Credit £
20XX				
5 Feb	Land and buildings	GL001	81,000	
	Bank/cash	GL002		81,000
			81,000	81,000
Being purchase of new factory building				

Note that the reference column would be used to enter the general ledger code for the accounts being debited and credited.

Carried out £10,000 of building work in order to make the building suitable for the manufacturing process, paid in cash

Date	Account	Ref	Debit £	Credit £
20XX				
5 Feb	Land and buildings	GL001	10,000	
	Bank/cash	GL002		10,000
			10,000	10,000
Being alterations to new factory				

Purchased a TV1 machine for £4,000 cash which was installed by Harris's own employees using £200 of materials and incurring wages costs of £600

Date	Account	Ref	Debit £	Credit £
20XX				
5 Feb	Machinery	GL003	4,800	
	Bank/cash	GL002		4,000
	Purchases	GL100		200
	Wages	GL002		600
			4,800	4,800
Being purchase and installation of TV1 machine				

Redecorated a building that was already owned and is used for the sales and administration departments at a total cost of £1,400, paid in cash

Date	Account	Ref	Debit £	Credit £
20XX				
5 Feb	Buildings maintenance	GL110	1,400	
	Bank/cash	GL002		1,400
			1,400	1,400
Being redecoration of sales and administration department building				

Purchased a computer to help in the administration department for £1,200 together with computer software costing £400. The cost of the computer included £50 of CDs and £20 of printer paper that were delivered with it. All transactions were paid in cash

Date	Account	Ref	Debit £	Credit £
20XX				
5 Feb	Computers	GL004	1,530	
	Stationery	GL120	70	
	Bank/cash	GL002		1,600
			1,600	1,600
Being purchase of computer				

Employed contract cleaners to clean the new TV1 machine after its first week of operation at a cost of £150, paid in cash

Date	Account	Ref	Debit £	Credit £
20XX				
5 Feb	Cleaning costs	GL130	150	
	Bank/cash	GL002		150
			150	150
Being cleaning of TV1 week 1				

Purchased a new delivery van at a cost of £16,400 which included £100 of delivery charges and £200 of road fund licence, all paid in cash

Date	Account	Ref	Debit £	Credit £
20XX				
5 Feb	Motor vehicles	GL005	16,200	
	Motor expenses	GL140	200	
	Bank/cash	GL002		16,400
			16,400	16,400
Being purchase of new delivery van				

Purchased some office furniture for £1,300 on credit

Date	Account	Ref	Debit £	Credit £
20XX				
5 Feb	Furniture and fittings	GL006	1,300	
	Purchases ledger control	GL007		1,300
			1,300	1,300
Being purchase of office furniture				

Purchased a car for £15,000, paying £10,000 cash and receiving a part exchange allowance of £5,000 on an old car which it traded in

Date	Account	Ref	Debit £	Credit £
20XX				
5 Feb	Motor vehicles	GL005	15,000	
	Bank/cash	GL002		10,000
	Disposal	GL008		5,000
			15,000	15,000
Being purchase of new car for cash/part exchange				

Task 3

A business has recently purchased four cars for use by its sales force at a total invoiced amount of £79,600. This total includes £400 of delivery charges and £800 of road fund licences. The amount due was paid by cheque upon delivery of the cars.

Draft the journal entry for the acquisition of these cars.

Account name	Amount £	Debit (✓)	Credit (✓)

AUTHORISATION FOR NON-CURRENT ASSET ACQUISITIONS

Clearly the acquisition of non-current assets is a major cost to a business and therefore it must be monitored and controlled. When a non-current asset is required by the business there is normally a strict procedure to follow:

- Acquisition application
- Price quotations
- Authorisation of application
- Monitoring of ongoing costs

Acquisition application

If an area of a business needs a new non-current asset then this requirement will need to be justified to the owners / managers of the business. The procedure for applying to acquire a new non-current asset will depend upon the nature and the cost of the asset and the organisation and size of the business.

- The application to buy a desk and chair for a new employee in the accounts department may well be a simple memo to the accountant

- The application to purchase a new piece of machinery costing £120,000 is likely to require a much more formal application with many details supporting the need for this acquisition. In larger businesses such applications will probably be dealt with by a capital expenditure committee or at the very least by a meeting of the senior management of the business

Price quotations

As with any purchase that a business makes, when purchasing a non-current asset it is important that the best possible combination of price, quality and service is found. This may well involve getting detailed quotations from a number of different suppliers. These quotations are likely to differ on price as well as the terms of after-sales service and the quality of the product. All of this will be relevant to the managers of the business who will make the decision as to whether to authorise this acquisition.

Authorisation

When considering whether or not to authorise the acquisition the business's management will not only consider the cost of the asset and the terms that are being offered. Many other considerations also go into the authorisation process.

- Can we afford the asset? The question here is whether the business has enough money to buy the asset (different funding methods will be considered later in this chapter)

- What effect will the new asset have upon staffing levels? A major new production line could mean that new employees are required. A sophisticated computer system may mean that a specialist has to be employed

- New machinery or technology may mean that staff will need to be trained in order to be able to operate the machinery or understand the technology

- What effect will there be on productivity? If a new machine or production line is acquired will this increase production each hour or day?

- What will be the effect on profitability? Is the asset worthwhile? Its costs and benefits have to be considered over a number of years in order to determine whether it will add to the business or detract from it

Monitoring of ongoing costs

Many capital acquisitions that a business makes will not be one-off purchases but rather an ongoing development over time. For example, if a new factory is being built and stocked with machinery this may well take a number of months. When the initial purchase application was approved the business's management will have had a price quotation for the job but it is important that all aspects of the job are monitored over time to ensure that there are no unforeseen cost overruns.

METHODS OF FUNDING

We have already seen that the acquisition of non-current assets is a major expense for any business. You need to know about the different methods of funding the acquisition, but you only need to know the detailed double entry for cash, credit and part exchange transactions, which we covered earlier in this chapter.

Cash/Credit purchase

The most obvious choice is a CASH PURCHASE where the asset is paid for at the time of transaction or a CREDIT PURCHASE where payment is made at a later date (for example within 30 days of the invoice date). In both instances the business purchasing the asset will need to have the funds available, either immediately or within the credit period.

Many businesses will not have enough funds in their bank account to purchase such assets with cash or on normal commercial credit terms. Therefore alternative options have to be considered.

Borrowing

Businesses may borrow the money to acquire new non-current assets either by a LOAN or a MORTGAGE. Loans are available from banks, building societies and many other providers of finance. A loan for the purchase of a non-current asset will normally be for a non-current amount for any period of time up to about ten years. Interest will be charged on the amount outstanding and the loan will normally be repaid by monthly or quarterly instalments.

A mortgage is a specific type of loan which might be a more suitable method of borrowing for the purchase of land and buildings. The mortgage loan can be for any amount up to 95% of the value of the property and can be repaid over a period of up to 25 years. The property serves as security for the loan in case the repayments are not made. Interest and capital will normally be paid in monthly instalments.

For any loan the interest charged will appear in the profit and loss account (statement of profit or loss) as an expense each year and the outstanding amount of the loan will appear on the statement of financial position as a long term liability.

Hire purchase or finance lease

Many non-current assets such as motor vehicles, machinery, office equipment and computers can be purchased under a HIRE PURCHASE AGREEMENT or FINANCE LEASE.

Under these arrangements the business pays an initial deposit to the finance company and from that point onwards has full use of the asset although the asset remains, in legal terms, the property of the finance company. The business makes regular payments to the finance company, usually monthly or quarterly, which are designed to pay off the capital cost of the asset plus the interest charged by the finance company. At the end of a hire purchase period the asset legally becomes owned by the business. At the end of a finance lease period there is normally no option to purchase the asset.

The interest element of the repayments appears in the profit and loss account as an expense. Although the non-current asset is not legally owned by the business, best accounting practice is that it appears in the statement of financial position as a non-current asset at its cost as if it had been purchased outright. There will also be a creditor for the amount still owed to the finance company.

Part exchange

A part exchange deal to part-fund an acquisition is very common, particularly in the motor trade. If the business wishes to purchase a new asset it can offer an old asset in PART EXCHANGE. In the case of a car the car dealer will place a value on the old car and deduct this value from the cost of the new car so the business needs only to pay the difference.

Task 4

A business purchases a new car costing £25,000, paying £15,000 in cash and receiving £10,000 as part exchange for an old car traded in.

Draft the journal entry for the this transaction (ignore VAT) and provide the narrative.

Account name	Amount £	Debit (✓)	Credit (✓)

RECORDING ACQUISITIONS IN THE NON-CURRENT ASSET REGISTER

As we have already seen it is important that a business has strict control over its non-current assets. In order to keep track of all of them most businesses will keep a NON-CURRENT ASSET REGISTER or FIXED ASSET REGISTER. For each non-current asset that the business acquires a detailed record will be kept in the register, typically showing the following:

- A description of the asset and possibly an asset number

- Its physical location within the business

- The supplier and the date of purchase

- The cost of the asset

- The estimated lifespan of the asset

- Any estimated scrap value of the asset at the end of its life

- The method of depreciation to be applied (see Chapter 4)

- The depreciation percentage

- The amount of depreciation charged each year

- The accumulated depreciation at the end of each year

- The carrying amount of the asset at the end of each year (see Chapter 4)

- Eventually the details of the disposal of the asset including sale proceeds and any profit or loss on disposal (see Chapter 5)

HOW IT WORKS

Kendall Engineering has just purchased a new machine, the FD254, from Leyland Machinery for £120,000. Today's date is 1 March 20XX and the machine is allocated asset number 02635. The machine is located in the factory and is expected to be used for five years after which it will have an estimated scrap value of £20,000.

We will now enter these initial details in the non-current asset register. In Chapters 4 and 5 the remaining entries in the non-current asset register will be considered.

Non-current asset number 02635
Description Machine FD254
Location Factory
Supplier **Leyland Machinery**

Acquisition date	Cost £	Expected life (years)	Estimated residual value £	Depreciation method	Depreciation rate	Depreciation charge for the year £	Acc dep at end of the year £	Carrying amount at end of year £	Disposal proceeds £	Profit or loss on disposal £
20X7 1 Mar	120,000	5	20,000							

CHAPTER OVERVIEW

- Capital expenditure is the cost of acquiring non-current assets – assets for long-term use in the business rather than for sale

- Revenue expenditure is all other business expenditure

- The costs to be included as the cost of a non-current asset are the costs involved in purchasing the asset and getting it into working order – these are then included in the statement of financial position as non-current assets

- Revenue expenditure is charged to the statement of profit or loss as an expense

- The double entry for acquiring a non-current asset is to debit the relevant non-current asset account and to credit either bank or the purchases ledger control account depending upon whether the asset was purchased for cash or on credit

- If a non-current asset has been made or installed by the business's own workforce then the materials and wages costs are debited to the non-current asset account and credited to purchases and wages respectively

- The entries to the ledger accounts are often initiated by a journal entry instructing the bookkeeper to account for the acquisition of the non-current assets where these are bought on credit or using part exchange

- Control and monitoring of non-current assets is extremely important and a non-current asset should only be acquired if its acquisition application is authorised

- Many non-current assets will not be acquired for cash but will be financed by a loan or purchased on a hire purchase agreement

- Old assets can often be given in part-exchange for a new asset in order to reduce the cost of the new asset

- The details of all non-current assets will be kept in a non-current asset register

Keywords

Non-current assets – assets acquired for long-term use within the business

Capital expenditure – expenditure on acquiring non-current assets

Revenue expenditure – all other non-capital expenditure – therefore any expenditure that is not the acquisition or major improvement of non-current assets

Capitalised – when the cost of a non-current asset is included in the statement of financial position (SFP)

Capitalisation policy – the business's policy for determining when capital expenditure is capitalised

Acquisition application – an application by an area of the business to purchase a non-current asset

Loan – a fixed amount borrowed from a bank or building society etc which is to be repaid over a fixed period of time on which interest is paid on the outstanding amount

Mortgage – a specific type of loan for the purchase of buildings where the building itself acts as security for the loan

Hire purchase agreement – a method of financing the purchase of a non-current asset where an initial deposit is paid to the finance company followed by a fixed number of instalments after which the asset is owned by the business

Finance lease – a method of financing the purchase of a non-current asset which is very similar to a hire purchase agreement but where there is normally no option to purchase the asset at the end of the lease term

Part exchange – a method of reducing the cost of a new asset by offering an old asset in part exchange

Non-current asset register – a record of the details of all of the non-current assets of the business individually

BPP
LEARNING MEDIA

TEST YOUR LEARNING

Test 1

For each of the following transactions state the amounts that should be treated as capital expenditure and the amounts that should be treated as revenue expenditure.

(a) A machine is purchased on credit at a total cost of £15,800. This includes delivery costs of £350, installation costs of £550 and a supply of lubricating oil for the machine costing £100

Capital expenditure   £ [   ]

Revenue expenditure   £ [   ]

(b) A building plot is purchased for £60,000 plus surveyor's fees of £600 and legal fees of £500

Capital expenditure   £ [   ]

Revenue expenditure   £ [   ]

(c) A new computer system is installed at a cost of £65,000. The computer room has had to be re-wired for this system at a cost of £3,600 and, while the electricians were in the building, the sales department lighting system was repaired at a cost of £800

Capital expenditure   £ [   ]

Revenue expenditure   £ [   ]

Test 2

Draft journal entries for each of the following non-current asset acquisitions.

(a) Desks and chairs for the head office at a cost of £4,200, paid for by cheque

Account name	Amount £	Debit (✓)	Credit (✓)

(b) A new computer purchased on credit at a total cost of £2,400 including £100 of rewritable CDs

Account name	Amount £	Debit (✓)	Credit (✓)

(c) A new machine purchased at a cost of £9,600 by cheque and installed by the business's own employees using materials costing £200 and incurring wages costs of £800

Account name	Amount £	Debit (✓)	Credit (✓)

Test 3

If a machine is purchased under a hire purchase agreement when would it appear as a non-current asset in the business's statement of financial position?

(✓)

On the date of payment of the deposit ☐

On the date of the final instalment ☐

Never ☐

chapter 4:
DEPRECIATION OF
NON-CURRENT ASSETS

chapter coverage 📖

In this chapter we consider the detailed accounting treatment for non-current assets. They are recorded in the statement of financial position at their original cost but this cost must be charged over time to the statement of profit or loss because the assets are being used to earn revenues for the business. This method of charging the cost of non-current assets to the statement of profit or loss is known as depreciation.

The topics covered are:

✍ What is depreciation?

✍ Methods of calculating depreciation

✍ Straight line method

✍ Diminishing balance method

✍ Choice of method

✍ Depreciation policies

✍ Accounting for depreciation

✍ Depreciation and the non-current asset register

WHAT IS DEPRECIATION?

We will start with the technical definition of DEPRECIATION from the International Accounting Standard IAS 16 (Property, plant and equipment):

'Depreciation is the systematic allocation of the cost of an asset less its residual value over its useful life.'

Depreciation therefore refers to the accounting concept of **accruals**. When a non-current asset is purchased its entire cost is included in the relevant asset account and is then recorded as a non-current asset in the statement of financial position. According to the accruals concept all of the costs involved in producing the income of the business during a period should be charged to the statement of profit and loss as an expense in the same period. Non-current assets that are used in the business are earning income for the business over several accounting periods, so a part of their cost should be charged to the statement of profit and loss in each accounting period in order to accord with the accruals concept – this is the depreciation charge.

Estimating how much of the cost to allocate in each accounting period will depend on the asset and on how it is used by the business to generate profit, for example:

- Machinery, motor vehicles and furniture will tend to wear out through use

- Leases on buildings will be consumed by the passage of time as the lease term diminishes

- Computer equipment becomes obsolete as technology advances

The aim of depreciation therefore is to charge or allocate the asset's cost to the statement of profit and loss of each accounting period of its useful life as an expense in order to match with the income that the asset has earned in the period.

The only type of non-current asset that does not have to be depreciated is freehold land. Since it has an infinite life it is not consumed in the business.

If some of the asset's cost has been consumed then the asset is 'worth' less than its original cost. This is reflected in the statement of financial position where non-current assets are shown at their cost less all of the depreciation charged to date.

This is known under international standards as the CARRYING AMOUNT of the non-current asset.

COST	–	DEPRECIATION TO DATE	=	CARRYING AMOUNT

METHODS OF CALCULATING DEPRECIATION

The amount of depreciation on a non-current asset that is allocated to the statement of profit or loss each year is just an estimate of how much of the asset's cost has been used up in generating profit during the year. In order to make such estimates businesses will have DEPRECIATION POLICIES that state the method to be used for depreciation of each type of non-current asset. This method should generally be used every year in order to be **consistent**.

The two methods of depreciation that are assessable in Accounts Preparation are:

- The straight line method
- The diminishing balance method

STRAIGHT LINE METHOD

The aim of the STRAIGHT LINE METHOD of depreciation is to charge the same amount of depreciation on the non-current asset in each year of the asset's life.

To calculate the depreciation charge for a non-current asset under this method we need to know:

- The COST of the asset – see Chapter 3

- Its USEFUL LIFE – this is the time period over which it is estimated that the non-current asset will be used within the business

- Its RESIDUAL VALUE – this is the scrap value that it is expected the asset can be sold for when its useful life is over

Depreciation using the straight line method can be calculated using:

- A percentage of the asset's cost less residual value
- A fraction of the asset's cost less residual value
- A period of time

The calculated depreciation for one year is then added to any depreciation charged in previous years and deducted from the asset's acquisition cost to arrive at its carrying amount in the statement of financial position.

HOW IT WORKS

Nick Waldron has recently set up a retail venture known as N W Traders. One of the non-current assets that has been purchased is an item of machinery that cost £8,000 and which Nick estimates will be used in the business for eight years. After this date it will need to be replaced due to technological changes, and it will have no resale (residual) value at that date. The machine is to be depreciated using the straight line method.

Using the **period of time method**, the annual depreciation charge is calculated as:

$$\frac{\text{Asset's acquisition cost}}{\text{Asset's estimated useful life}}$$

The depreciation charge for this asset will be:

$$\frac{£8,000}{8 \text{ years}} = £1,000 \text{ per year}$$

The same information allows us to calculate depreciation using the **percentage method**. If the asset is held for eight years then in each year $1/8 \times 100\% = 12.5\%$ of the cost is charged in each year. This comes out at £8,000 × 12.5% = £1,000 per year.

Again the same information is used to calculate depreciation using the **fraction method**. If the asset is held for eight years then in each year $1/8^{th}$ of the cost is charged, that is £8,000 × 1/8 = £1,000 per year.

Whichever method of calculation is used, we can see that in each year:

- £1,000 will be charged to the statement of profit or loss as an expense

- £1,000 will be deducted from the cost of the non-current asset in the statement of financial position to arrive at its carrying amount

At the end of the first year the carrying amount will be £8,000 – £1,000 = £7,000. At the end of the asset's estimated useful life its carrying amount will be:

Cost – Depreciation to date

£8,000 – (8 × £1,000) = nil

Task 1

Using the non-current asset details given above what will be the carrying amount of the asset after it has been owned by N W Traders for three years?

£ [   ]

Residual value

In the previous example we were told that the asset would be worthless by the end of its useful life. However many non-current assets that a business purchases are likely to be sold on in the second-hand market at the end of their useful life to the business. This is probably especially the case with motor vehicles which may be kept for three or four years and then replaced. Such assets will have a resale value at the date of their sale.

With the straight line depreciation method, when the non-current asset is purchased we need to estimate:

- The asset's useful life and

- Its scrap value or resale value at the end of the useful life, known as the asset's RESIDUAL VALUE

The amount that is to be depreciated over the asset's useful life is then:

COST	–	RESIDUAL VALUE

HOW IT WORKS

N W Traders has also purchased a motor van for deliveries for £16,000. It is estimated that the van will be used for three years and then sold for £5,500.

The relevant figures for this non-current asset are therefore:

Cost   £16,000
Useful life   3 years
Residual value   £5,500

Using the straight line period of time method of depreciation, the annual charge for depreciation will be:

$$\frac{\text{Cost} - \text{Residual value}}{\text{Useful life}} = \frac{£16,000 - £5,500}{3 \text{ years}}$$

$$= £3,500 \text{ per year}$$

At the end of each year of the van's life this is how it will appear at its net book value in the statement of financial position (SFP):

End of Year 1	£16,000 – £3,500	=	£12,500
End of Year 2	£16,000 – (2 × £3,500)	=	£9,000
End of Year 3	£16,000 – (3 × £3,500)	=	£5,500

Task 2

A business has purchased a non-current asset for £22,000 which has a useful life of four years and a residual value at the end of this period of £9,000.

What is the annual depreciation charge using the straight line method?

£ [   ]

What is the carrying amount of the asset after two years?

£ [   ]

DIMINISHING BALANCE METHOD

The aim of the DIMINISHING BALANCE METHOD of depreciation is to have a higher charge for depreciation in the early years of the non-current asset's life and a lower charge in later years. This reflects the pattern of consumption or loss of value to the business of certain assets, such as motor vehicles, that tend to lose more of their value in the early years of their life. Note that the value to the business may be quite different from any market value an asset may have.

To calculate the annual depreciation charge using the diminishing balance method we use a fixed percentage rate.

- In the first year the percentage is applied to the **cost** of the asset
- In subsequent years the percentage is applied to the asset's **carrying amount** as at the beginning of the period

Determining the percentage rate is a complicated calculation which you do not need to carry out – you will be given the percentage rate to use.

This method is sometimes referred to as the REDUCING BALANCE method.

HOW IT WORKS

N W Traders has purchased a motor van for deliveries for £16,000 which it will use for three years and then sell for £5,500.

This van is to be depreciated under the diminishing balance method at a rate of 30% per annum.

	£	Annual depreciation charge £
Original cost	16,000	
Year 1 depreciation £16,000 × 30%	4,800	4,800
NBV at end of Year 1	11,200	
Year 2 depreciation £11,200 × 30%	3,360	3,360
NBV at end of Year 2	7,840	
Year 3 depreciation £7,840 × 30%	2,352	2,352
NBV at end of Year 3	5,488	

Note that:

- The depreciation charge is higher in year 1 and subsequently decreases

- The calculations have brought the carrying amount of the asset down to approximately its residual value, £5,500, at the end of its three year useful life

Task 3

A business has purchased a non-current asset for £22,000 which has a useful life of four years and a residual value at the end of this period of £9,000. It is to be depreciated using the diminishing balance method at a rate of 20%.

What is the depreciation charge for each year of the asset's life, and the asset's carrying amount at the end of each year?

	Depreciation charge £	Carrying amount £
Year 1		
Year 2		
Year 3		
Year 4		

CHOICE OF METHOD

IAS 16 allows businesses to choose the method of depreciation that is most appropriate to their non-current assets. Most businesses will choose different depreciation methods and rates for different types of asset.

- The **straight line** method is often used for assets that are likely to be kept for their entire useful lives and to have low expected resale values, such as machinery and office furniture and fittings

- The **diminishing balance** method is usually found to be more appropriate for assets such as motor vehicles that lose more of their value to the business in early years and are likely to be sold before the end of their possible lives

DEPRECIATION POLICIES

Once the depreciation method and rates have been set they should be kept under review but should only be changed for a good reason. This is in order to comply with the accounting concept of **consistency** which states that items in the accounting records should be dealt with in the same manner each year.

Depreciation on classes of asset

In the examples so far we have seen how to calculate the depreciation for an individual non-current asset by looking at its cost, its useful life and its residual value. You also need to be able to calculate the depreciation charge for the year for an entire class of assets. In order to do this in an assessment you will be told the depreciation policy for that class of non-current asset.

HOW IT WORKS

Harris Incorporated has a number of different classes of non-current asset, including buildings and motor vehicles. The depreciation policies for these two classes of asset are:

- Buildings – straight line method at 2% per year
- Motor vehicles – 25% using the diminishing balance method

To determine the depreciation charge for each class of non-current asset for the year certain information is required.

- As the buildings are being depreciated using the straight line method we need to know the cost of the buildings at the end of the year. Let us suppose this is £100,000

- For the motor vehicles the policy is to use the diminishing balance method and therefore we need the figure for the carrying amount of the motor vehicles at the end of the year. In this case let us suppose this is £40,000

The depreciation charge for the year for each class of non-current assets is therefore:

Buildings	£100,000 × 2%	=	£2,000
Motor vehicles	£ 40,000 × 25%	=	£10,000

Assets purchased during the year

If non-current assets are purchased part of the way through the year then the business has a choice: it can depreciate the new asset for the whole year or it can depreciate it only for the period since it was acquired.

This choice will be set out in the depreciation policy. The two alternatives are normally expressed as follows:

'A full year's depreciation charge is made in the year of acquisition and none in the year of disposal' – this means that no matter when the new asset was purchased during the year, a full year's depreciation is charged in that year, but no charge is made in the year of disposal irrespective of when in that year the asset was disposed of. Disposals of non-current assets are discussed in more detail in Chapter 5.

'Depreciation is calculated on an annual basis and charged in equal instalments for each full month an asset is owned in the year' – here, the depreciation charge must be based on the number of months in the year that the asset has actually been owned. Therefore it will need to be calculated on a pro-rata basis.

HOW IT WORKS

Two businesses purchase a piece of machinery on 1 April 20XX for £20,000 and both businesses have an accounting period which runs from 1 January to 31 December.

Business A depreciates its machinery at 10% using the straight line method with a full year's charge in the year of acquisition.

Business B depreciates its machinery at 10% per annum on the straight line basis.

The depreciation charges for each business in the year of acquisition for this machinery is:

A	£20,000 × 10%	=	£2,000
B	£20,000 × 10% × 9/12	=	£1,500 (as the asset has only been owned for 9 months of the year)

ACCOUNTING FOR DEPRECIATION

Accounting entries for the annual depreciation charge reflect the treatment of depreciation that we have already discussed.

Each year the statement of profit or loss is charged with the DEPRECIATION CHARGE for the year. This is a **debit in the depreciation charge account**.

ACCUMULATED DEPRECIATION that has been charged to date on the non-current assets is deducted from their cost to give the carrying amount – this accumulated depreciation is sometimes known as the PROVISION FOR DEPRECIATION. Therefore the depreciation for the year is entered as **a credit in the accumulated depreciation account**.

> Debit   Depreciation charge account
> Credit Accumulated depreciation account

Note that there are no entries to the non-current asset at cost account. This contains the original cost and it is not changed.

HOW IT WORKS

We shall now return to N W Traders who purchased a motor van for deliveries for £16,000 with a useful life of three years and a residual value of £5,500. The annual depreciation charge calculated using the straight line method is:

$$\frac{£16,000 - 5,500}{3 \text{ years}} = £3,500$$

We will record this in the ledger accounts for each of the three years (in practice the book of prime entry to record these entries is the journal).

Year 1

The depreciation charge of £3,500 is debited to the depreciation charge account and credited to the accumulated depreciation account.

Depreciation charge		
	£	£
Accumulated depreciation	3,500	

Accumulated depreciation

£		£
	Depreciation charge	3,500

At the end of Year 1 the depreciation charge account will be cleared to the statement of profit or loss as it is an expense item, so there will be no remaining balance on the account.

Depreciation charge

	£		£
Accumulated depreciation	3,500	SPL	3,500

The accumulated depreciation account however will appear in the statement of financial position and the balance will remain as the opening balance for Year 2.

Accumulated depreciation

	£		£
Year 1 Balance c/d	3,500	Year 1 Depreciation charge	3,500
		Year 2 Balance b/d	3,500

In the financial statements at the end of Year 1 the depreciation is treated as follows:

Statement of profit or loss Year 1

	£
Expenses:	
Depreciation charge	3,500

Statement of financial position Year 1

Non-current assets	Cost	Depreciation	Carrying amount
	£	£	£
Motor vehicles	16,000	3,500	12,500

Year 2

Year 2's depreciation charge of £3,500 is debited to the depreciation charge account and credited to the accumulated depreciation account.

Depreciation charge

	£		£
Accumulated depreciation	3,500		

Accumulated depreciation

	£		£
		Year 2 Balance b/d	3,500
		Year 2 Depreciation charge	3,500

At the end of Year 2 the depreciation charge account is once again cleared to the statement of profit or loss so there is no remaining balance on it.

Depreciation charge

	£		£
Accumulated depreciation	3,500	SPL	3,500

The accumulated depreciation account however will appear in the statement of financial position as the provision for depreciation, and its balance will remain as the opening balance for Year 3.

Provision for depreciation

	£		£
Year 2 Balance c/d	7,000	Year 2 Balance b/d	3,500
		Year 2 Depreciation charge	3,500
	7,000		7,000
		Year 3 Balance b/d	7,000

In the financial statements at the end of Year 2 depreciation is treated as follows:

Statement of profit or loss Year 2

Expenses:	£
Depreciation charge	3,500

Statement of financial position Year 2

Non-current assets	Cost	Depreciation	Carrying amount
	£	£	£
Motor vehicles	16,000	7,000	9,000

Year 3

The depreciation charge of £3,500 is debited to the depreciation charge account and credited to the accumulated depreciation account.

Depreciation charge

	£		£
Accumulated depreciation	3,500		

Accumulated depreciation

	£		£
		Year 3 Balance b/d	7,000
		Depreciation charge	3,500

At the end of the year the depreciation charge account is cleared to the statement of profit or loss so there is no remaining balance on it.

Depreciation charge

	£		£
Accumulated depreciation	3,500	SPL	3,500

The accumulated depreciation account however will appear in the statement of financial position and the balance will remain.

Accumulated depreciation

	£		£
Year 3 Balance c/d	10,500	Year 3 Balance b/d	7,000
		Year 3 Depreciation charge	3,500
	10,500		10,500
		Year 4 Balance b/d	10,500

In the financial statements at the end of Year 3 the depreciation is treated as follows:

Statement of profit or loss Year 3

Expenses:	£
Depreciation charge	3,500

Statement of financial position Year 3

Non-current assets	Cost	Depreciation	Carrying amount
	£	£	£
Motor vehicles	16,000	10,500	5,500

Task 4

A business which has just completed its first year trading has machinery costing £120,000. The depreciation policy is to depreciate machinery at the rate of 20% using the straight line method.

Show the ledger entries for the depreciation for the first year and the entries in the statement of profit or loss and statement of financial position at the end of the year.

Depreciation charge

	£		£

Accumulated depreciation

	£		£

Statement of profit or loss

Expenses:	£

Statement of financial position

Non-current assets	Cost £	Depreciation £	Carrying amount £
Machinery			

DEPRECIATION AND THE NON-CURRENT ASSET REGISTER

You will remember from Chapter 3 that all details for all non-current assets are kept in the non-current asset register. This includes entries for the annual depreciation charge and accumulated depreciation on each asset.

HOW IT WORKS

Kendall Engineering purchased a new machine, the FD254, from Leyland Machinery for £120,000 on 1 March 20X7. The machine is to be depreciated using the diminishing balance method at a rate of 30% per annum with a full year's charge in the year of purchase. The business's accounting year ends on 31 December.

It is now 31 December 20X7 and the entries relating to depreciation for the first year must be made. The charge is £120,000 × 30% = £36,000

NON-CURRENT ASSET REGISTER						
Non-current asset number		02635				
Description		Machine FD254				
Location		Factory				
Supplier		Leyland Machinery				
Acquisition date	*Cost £*	*Depreciation charge for the year £*	*Accumulated depreciation at end of the year*	*Carrying amount at end of year £*	*Disposal proceeds*	*Disposal date*
20X7						
1 Mar	120,000					
31 Dec		36,000	36,000	84,000		

Task 5

The diminishing balance method of accounting for depreciation gives the same amount of depreciation charged each year.

True [   ]

False [   ]

CHAPTER OVERVIEW

- Depreciation is a method of applying the accruals concept by charging some of the cost of non-current assets to the statement of profit or loss each year that they are used by the business

- The amount to be charged is an estimate of the amount of the cost that has been 'consumed' in the accounting period – this is estimated by calculating the depreciation charge either under the straight line method or the diminishing balance method

- The cost of the non-current asset minus the depreciation charged to date is known as the carrying amount (IAS) or net book value (UK GAAP)

- The straight line method of depreciation ensures that the same amount of depreciation is charged for each year of the asset's life

- Straight line depreciation is calculated as the cost of the asset less the residual value spread over the useful life of the asset

- The diminishing balance method of depreciation charges a larger amount of depreciation in the early years of the asset's life and a lower amount in the later years of its life

- Diminishing balance depreciation is calculated by applying a fixed percentage to the carrying amount of the non-current asset

- Care has to be taken over the precise depreciation policy of a business – some businesses charge a full year's depreciation on an asset no matter when it was purchased during the year, while other businesses charge depreciation only for the months that the asset has been owned in the first year

- When accounting for the depreciation charge it is debited to the depreciation charge account and credited to the accumulated depreciation account

- The depreciation charge account is cleared as an expense to the statement of profit or loss at the end of each year but the balance on the accumulated depreciation account is carried down as the opening balance for the following period

- The depreciation charge is shown as an expense in the statement of profit or loss

- The balance on the accumulated depreciation account is shown in the statement of financial position where it is deducted from the cost of the non-current asset to arrive at the carrying amount

- The depreciation method, rate, expense for the year, accumulated depreciation and carrying amount are all recorded in the non-current asset register

Keywords

Depreciation – the annual charge to the statement of profit or loss to reflect the use of the non-current asset during the period

Carrying amount – the cost of the non-current asset minus the depreciation charged to date over one or more years

Depreciation policies – the stated methods and rates of depreciation for a business

Straight line method – a method of calculating the depreciation charge to give the same amount of depreciation charge each year

Useful life – the period over which the business estimates that the non-current asset will be used

Residual value – the anticipated resale value of the non-current asset at the end of its useful life to the business

Diminishing balance method – method of calculating depreciation so that a larger amount is charged in the earlier years and smaller amounts in subsequent years

Depreciation charge – the amount of depreciation charged to the statement of profit or loss each year

Accumulated depreciation – the statement of financial position ledger account that records the accumulated depreciation to date on a non-current asset

Provision for depreciation – this is another name for the statement of financial position accumulated depreciation account

TEST YOUR LEARNING

Test 1

The main accounting concept underlying the depreciation of non-current assets is the materiality/consistency/accruals concept.

Test 2

A business has a machine that was purchased on 1 January 20X7 costing £11,500 with a useful life of five years and a residual value of £2,500. The policy is to depreciate machinery using the straight line method.

What is the depreciation charge for the year ended 31 December 20X8?

£ _____

What is the carrying amount of the machine at 31 December 20X8?

£ _____

Test 3

A business owns a car that was purchased on 1 January 20X7 for £16,400. It has a useful life of three years and a residual value of £4,500 at that date. The car is to be depreciated at 35% each year using the diminishing balance method.

What is the depreciation charge for the year ended 31 December 20X8?

£ _____

What is the carrying amount of the car at 31 December 20X8?

£ _____

Test 4

A business has machinery with a cost of £240,000 and depreciation to date at the start of the year of £135,000. The policy is to depreciate the machinery at the rate of 30% using the diminishing balance method.

What is this year's depreciation charge?

£ _____

Test 5

A business purchased a delivery lorry for £24,000 on 1 June 20XX which is to be depreciated using the straight line method at a rate of 20% per annum, charged in equal instalments for each full month an asset is owned.

What is the depreciation charge for the accounting year ending 31 December 20XX?

£ _____

chapter 5:
DISPOSAL OF NON-CURRENT ASSETS

---

chapter coverage 📖

Having considered the acquisition of non-current assets and their accounting treatment during their useful lives we must now consider the process of selling a non-current asset when it is of no more use to the business. In this chapter we also consider the relationship between the non-current asset register and the actual non-current assets held. At regular intervals the details of assets in the non-current asset register should be physically checked to the actual assets held on the premises.

The topics covered are:

✍ Accounting for disposals

✍ Profit and loss on disposal

✍ Part exchange of an asset

✍ Disposals and the non-current asset register

✍ Checking physical assets to the register

ACCOUNTING FOR DISPOSALS

When a non-current asset is sold there are two effects on the accounts of the business:

- All accounting entries for the asset must be removed from the accounting records

- Any profit or loss on the disposal of the asset must be calculated and accounted for

With regard to the general ledger all of this can be done in one ledger account – the DISPOSALS ACCOUNT.

The first step is to use the journal to remove the cost of the asset and the accumulated depreciation for that asset from the ledger accounts – these amounts are taken out of the relevant accounts and put into the disposals account:

Debit   Disposals account
Credit   Non-current asset at cost account

- With the original cost of the asset

Debit   Accumulated depreciation account
Credit   Disposals account

- With the accumulated depreciation on the asset up to the date of disposal

This has removed all traces of the asset sold from the general ledger accounts – now we must deal with the sale proceeds:

Debit   Bank/cash or Sales ledger control account
Credit   Disposals account

- With the sale proceeds – if a cheque is received then the bank account will be debited, if cash is received the cash account will be debited, and if the sale is made on credit then the sales ledger control account will be debited

The final step is to calculate the balance on the disposals account. This will be either a PROFIT ON DISPOSAL if there is a credit balance or a LOSS ON DISPOSAL if there is a debit balance. This will be credited to the statement of profit or loss as income if it is a profit, or debited as an expense if it is a loss.

The carrying amount of any asset that has been disposed of during an accounting period will always be shown as zero at the end of the period.

HOW IT WORKS

Harris Incorporated purchased a machine on 1 January 20X6 with a cheque for £15,000. This was to be depreciated using the straight line method at a rate of 20% per annum. The machine was sold for £5,000 on 31 December 20X8. The buyer paid by cheque.

Before we look at the accounting entries for this sale we will examine what has happened here. The machine was owned for the whole of 20X6, 20X7 and 20X8 and therefore had three years of depreciation charges at £3,000 (£15,000 × 20%) per annum.

	£
Cost of machine	15,000
Accumulated depreciation	9,000
Carrying amount at 31 December 20X8	6,000
Sale proceeds	5,000
Loss on sale	1,000

At the date of the disposal the machine had a carrying amount of £6,000 but was sold for only £5,000. Therefore a loss was made on the disposal of £1,000.

Now we will consider the accounting entries:

Debit   Disposals account
Credit   Non-current asset at cost account

- **With the original cost of the asset**

Machine at cost account

		£			£
20X6			20X8		
1 Jan	Bank/cash	15,000	31 Dec	Disposals	15,000

Disposals account

		£		£
20X8				
31 Dec	Machine	15,000		

Debit   Accumulated depreciation account
Credit   Disposals account

- **With the accumulated depreciation on the asset up to the date of sale**

Accumulated depreciation account

		£			£
20X6			20X6		
31 Dec	Balance c/d	3,000	31 Dec	Depreciation	3,000
		3,000			3,000
20X7			20X7		
31 Dec	Balance c/d	6,000	1 Jan	Balance b/d	3,000
		6,000	31 Dec	Depreciation	3,000
					6,000
20X8			20X8		
31 Dec	Disposals	9,000	1 Jan	Balance b/d	6,000
		9,000	31 Dec	Depreciation	3,000
					9,000

Disposals account

		£			£
20X8			20X8		
31 Dec	Machine	15,000	31 Dec	Accumulated depreciation	9,000

Debit   Bank/cash
Credit   Disposals account

- **With the sale proceeds**

Disposals account

		£			£
20X8			20X8		
31 Dec	Machine	15,000	31 Dec	Accumulated depreciation	9,000
			31 Dec	Bank/cash – proceeds	5,000

Finally, balance the disposals account to find the profit or the loss on disposal:

Disposals account

		£			£
20X8			20X8		
31 Dec	Machine	15,000	31 Dec	Accumulated depreciation	9,000
			31 Dec	Bank/cash – proceeds	5,000
			31 Dec	Loss	1,000
		15,000			15,000

To complete the double entry for this loss on disposal there is a credit in the disposals account and a debit (an expense) to the statement of profit or loss.

Task 1

A business purchased a motor car for £11,200 on 1 January 20X7 and this car was sold for £5,000 on 31 December 20X8. The depreciation policy for the motor car was 30% per annum on the diminishing balance basis, with a full year's charge in the year of disposal.

(a)   Calculate the carrying amount of the car on 31 December 20X8

£ [   ]

(b)   Determine any profit or loss that has been made on the disposal

£ [   ]

(c)   Write up the motor car at cost account, the accumulated depreciation on the motor car account and the disposals account

Motor car at cost account

	£		£

Accumulated depreciation on the motor car account

	£		£

Disposals account

	£		£

Date of disposal

Some care must be taken with the depreciation policy details when an asset is disposed of part way through the year. Depreciation should be charged on the asset up to the date of disposal according to the depreciation policy of the organisation.

HOW IT WORKS

Two businesses each purchase a machine on 1 August 20X6 for £3,600. Both businesses have an accounting period which runs from 1 January to 31 December. Both businesses sell their asset on 31 October 20X8 for £2,800.

Business A depreciates its machinery at 10% on the straight line basis with a full year's charge in the year of acquisition and none in the year of disposal.

Business B depreciates its machinery at 10% per annum on the straight line basis, charged in equal instalments for each full month an asset is owned in the year.

The profit or loss on disposal for each business is:

	Business A £		Business B £
Cost	3,600		3,600
Depreciation –			
to 31 December 20X6	(360)	× 5/12	(150)
to 31 December 20X7	(360)		(360)
to 31 October 20X8	–	× 10/12	(300)
Carrying amount	2,880		2,790
Sale proceeds	2,800		2,800
Loss on disposal	80	Profit	10

PROFIT AND LOSS ON DISPOSAL

A profit on disposal means that the proceeds received on the disposal of the asset are greater than the carrying amount of the asset at the date of disposal.

The aim of depreciation is to charge the cost of the asset (less its residual value if any) to the statement of profit or loss over its useful life. Consequently, if depreciation had been correctly charged over the asset's useful life, the carrying amount of the asset at the date of disposal would be equal to the sales proceeds (ie its actual residual value). In practice, of course, the depreciation charged is only the business's best estimate and therefore it is usual for either a profit or loss to arise on the disposal.

In effect a profit on disposal means that the asset has been OVER-DEPRECIATED ie the asset's cost has been reduced by depreciation to a carrying amount that is less than its actual residual value.

Similarly a loss on disposal means that the proceeds received on the disposal of the asset are less than the carrying amount of the asset at the date of disposal. Accordingly, a loss on disposal means that the asset has been UNDER-DEPRECIATED ie the asset's cost has not been sufficiently reduced by depreciation, and its carrying amount at the date of disposal is more than its actual residual value.

PART EXCHANGE OF AN ASSET

In many cases when a business is selling a non-current asset it will be in order to replace it with a new or newer model. This is often done by means of a PART EXCHANGE, most frequently in the case of motor vehicles.

This means that when the new asset is purchased the old asset is taken as part of the purchase price – a PART EXCHANGE ALLOWANCE is given on the old asset in order to reduce the cash price of the new asset. This part exchange allowance is therefore:

- Part of the cost of the new asset (as we saw in Chapter 3) as well as the cash that is also paid

- Effectively the disposal proceeds of the old asset

There are no cash proceeds for the sale of the old asset but the part exchange allowance is treated as the sale proceeds as follows:

Debit   Non-current asset at cost account for the new asset
Credit   Disposals account

- **With the part exchange allowance**

The asset's cost and accumulated depreciation are removed from their respective accounts and entered into the disposals account as well, as in a normal disposal for cash.

The credit to the disposals account allows us to calculate a profit or loss on disposal by comparing the part exchange allowance with the carrying amount.

The debit to the non-current asset at cost account recognises that the part exchange allowance is part of the cost of the new asset together with the remainder of the cash cost, as we saw in Chapter 3.

HOW IT WORKS

Harris Incorporated is buying a new car for an employee with a list price of £12,000. The car dealer has agreed to take the employee's old car in part exchange with a part exchange allowance of £3,800.

The old car cost £13,500 on 1 January 20X6. At the date of disposal, 30 June 20X8, there was accumulated depreciation charged to it of £9,250.

The profit or loss on disposal of the old car can first be calculated:

	£
Cost	13,500
Accumulated depreciation	9,250
Carrying amount	4,250
Part exchange allowance	3,800
Loss on disposal	450

The cash to be paid for the new car can also be calculated:

	£
List price	12,000
Less part exchange allowance	(3,800)
Cash payable	8,200

Now we will deal with the entries in the ledger accounts:

Motor car at cost account

		£			£
20X6			20X8		
1 Jan	Bank/cash	13,500	30 Jun	Disposals	13,500
20X8			20X8		
30 Jun	Bank/cash	8,200	30 Jun	Balance c/d	12,000
30 Jun	Disposals	3,800			
		12,000			12,000
1 Jul	Balance b/d	12,000			

Note that the cost of the old car has been removed and taken to the disposals account and the cost of the new car in full, £12,000, has been entered into the account by making two entries, one from the bank/cash account for the cash payable and one from the disposals account for the part exchange allowance.

Motor car accumulated depreciation account

		£			£
20X8			20X8		
30 Jun	Disposals	9,250	30 Jun	Balance b/d	9,250

Disposals account

		£			£
20X8			20X8		
30 Jun	Motor car at cost	13,500	30 Jun	Motor car accumulated depreciation	9,250
			30 Jun	Motor car at cost – allowance	3,800
			30 Jun	Loss on disposal	450
		13,500			13,500

Task 2

A business purchased a car on 1 March 20X6 for £10,000. This car was part exchanged for a new one with a total list price of £11,000 on 31 May 20X8. At that date the old car had had £5,500 of accumulated depreciation charged to it. The part exchange allowance given on the old car was £4,800.

Show the accounting entries necessary to record the sale of the old car and purchase of the new car.

Car at cost account

	£		£

Car accumulated depreciation account

	£		£

Disposals account

	£		£

DISPOSALS AND THE NON-CURRENT ASSET REGISTER

We have already seen how entries should be made in the non-current asset register when an asset is purchased and in each year of its life to record the depreciation. When a non-current asset is sold the register is then completed with entries being made for the disposal proceeds and any profit or loss on disposal. Once the profit or loss on disposal has been recorded in the register the asset is effectively removed from the register.

HOW IT WORKS

We saw in Chapter 4 that an FD254 machine was purchased by Kendall Engineering for £120,000 on 1 March 20X7. It is being depreciated at 30% diminishing balance with a full year's charge in the year of acquisition but none in the year of disposal. Let us now complete the picture by supposing that this machine was sold on 1 February 20X9 for £50,000. Kendall Engineering has a 31 December year end.

In the register we need to record the disposal and remove the asset by entering:

- The date of disposal (1 Feb 20X9)
- The disposal proceeds (£50,000) and
- The profit or loss on disposal (£50,000 – £58,800 = £8,800 loss)

Non-current asset register						
Non-current asset number			02635			
Description			Machine FD254			
Location			Factory			
Supplier			Leyland Machinery			
Date	Cost £	Depreciation charge for the year £	Accumulated depreciation at end of the year £	Carrying amount at end of year £	Disposal proceeds	Profit or loss on disposal £
20X7 1 Mar	120,000					
31 Dec		36,000	36,000	84,000		
31 Dec 20X8		25,200	61,200	58,800	31 Dec 20X8	31 Dec 20X8
31 Dec 20X9					50,000	(8,800)

Task 3

On 1 May 20X5 Kendall Engineering purchased from Leyland Machinery a fork lift truck type XC355 which is used in the warehouse for £34,000. The truck was given the asset number 24116 and was estimated to have a useful life of four years and a residual value of £6,250.

The truck is depreciated at 30% using the diminishing balance method with a full year's charge in the year of acquisition and none in the year of disposal. The business's year end is 31 December. The truck was sold on 20 March 20X8 for £10,500.

Make all the entries required for this truck in the non-current asset register given below.

NON-CURRENT ASSET REGISTER
Non-current asset number
Description
Location
Supplier

Date	Cost £	Expected life (years)	Estimated residual value	Depreciation method	Depreciation rate	Depreciation charge for the year £	Acc dep at end of the year £	Carrying amount at end of year £	Disposal proceeds £	Profit or loss on disposal £

CHECKING PHYSICAL ASSETS TO THE REGISTER

The main reason for keeping the non-current asset register is to help in the control of the non-current assets of a business. These are often very expensive items and in some cases, such as laptops, are also easily portable. Once a non-current asset has been purchased by the business it is important to check that it is still physically within the business on a fairly regular basis.

Physical checks can be made in two ways:

- Check that every non-current asset in the register still exists somewhere in the business
- Check that every non-current asset in the business is recorded in the register

It is unlikely that all the business's non-current assets will be physically checked at the same time in this manner but most businesses will have a rolling policy of checking categories of asset regularly so that all assets are checked once a year.

This physical check of the assets may show that there are some unusual features or discrepancies:

- Some assets that exist in the business may not be in the register – this means that when the asset was purchased no entries were made for the asset in the register
- Some entries in the register may not be up to date – for instance, the depreciation charge each year may not have been entered
- There may be no physical asset when one is recorded in the register – this may mean that an asset has been sold or scrapped but the disposal has not been recorded in the register, or it may mean the asset has been destroyed or stolen

Any unusual features or discrepancies found when carrying out this physical check must be reported to management to be dealt with appropriately.

Task 4

Which of the following reasons explains why an asset that is in use by the business does not appear in the non-current asset register?

A   The asset has been stolen

B   Depreciation has not been charged

C   The asset's carrying amount is zero

D   No entry was made in the register when the asset was purchased

---

CHAPTER OVERVIEW

- It is as important to control and authorise the disposal of non-current assets as it is their acquisition

- Accounting for the disposal takes place in the disposals account by entering the original cost and accumulated depreciation on the asset being disposed of together with the disposal proceeds

- The final balance on the disposal account will be either a profit on disposal – to be credited to the statement of profit or loss – or a loss on disposal, to be debited to the statement of profit or loss

- A profit on disposal represents over-depreciation and a loss on disposal represents under-depreciation

- In some cases a non-current asset will be disposed of by it being part exchanged in the purchase of a replacement asset – the part exchange allowance is treated as the disposal proceeds of the old asset and as part of the cost of the new asset

- When a non-current asset is disposed of the date of disposal, proceeds and the profit or loss should be recorded in the non-current asset register

- On a regular basis the physical non-current assets that a business has should be checked to the entries in the non-current asset register – any discrepancies should be reported to the appropriate person in the organisation for any required action to be taken

Keywords

Disposals account – the ledger account used to record all aspects of the disposal of the non-current asset

Profit or loss on disposal – the difference between the carrying amount of the asset at the date of disposal and the sale proceeds

Over-depreciation – results in a profit on disposal

Under-depreciation – results in a loss on disposal

Part exchange – a method of disposal whereby the old asset is given in part exchange for a new asset

Part exchange allowance – the value assigned to the old asset being part exchanged by the supplier of the new asset

TEST YOUR LEARNING

Test 1

A business purchases a computer on 1 April 20X5 for £2,200. This is then sold on 14 May 20X8 for £200. The depreciation policy is to depreciate computers on a diminishing balance basis at a rate of 40% with a full year's charge in the year of acquisition and none in the year of disposal. The business's accounting year ends on 31 December.

(a) Calculate the profit or loss on the sale of this computer.

£ [   ]

(b) Show all of the accounting entries for this computer from the date of purchase through to the date of sale.

Computer at cost account

	£		£

Computer accumulated depreciation account

	£		£

Disposals account

	£		£

Test 2

A business purchases a machine on 1 October 20X6 for £7,200 and this machine is then sold on 31 July 20X8 for £3,800. The machine is depreciated at a rate of 25% per annum on the straight line basis, charged in equal instalments for each full month an asset is owned in the year. The business's year end is 30 November.

(a) Calculate the profit or loss on the sale of this machine.

£ [   ]

(b) Show all of the accounting entries for this machine from the date of purchase through to the date of sale.

Machine at cost account

	£		£

Machine accumulated depreciation account

	£		£

Disposals account

	£		£

Test 3

(a) A loss on disposal can also be described as

over-depreciation/under-depreciation.

(b) A profit on disposal can also be described as

over-depreciation/under-depreciation.

Test 4

A business is purchasing a new motor van with a list price of £16,700 on 30 April 20X8. The car dealer has agreed to take an old motor van in part exchange requiring the business to pay only £12,200 for the new van. The old van had originally cost £13,600 on 1 July 20X5 and the accumulated depreciation on this van at 30 April 20X8 totalled £9,000.

Show the accounting entries required in the ledger accounts on 30 April 20X8 to deal with the purchase of this new van and the part exchange of the old van.

Van at cost account

	£		£

Van accumulated depreciation account

	£		£

Disposals account

	£		£

Test 5

A business purchases a computer with a serial number 1036525 for £4,800 from Timing Computers Ltd on 1 March 20X6. The computer is allocated an internal non-current asset number 10435 and is to be used in the sales department.

The computer is estimated to have a four year useful life and a residual value at the end of that period of just £600. It is to be depreciated using the diminishing balance method at a rate of 40% with a full year's charge in the year of acquisition and none in the year of disposal. The business's year end is 31 July.

On 27 June 20X8 the computer was sold for £700.

Record all of these details on the non-current asset register given.

NON-CURRENT ASSET REGISTER
Non-current asset number
Description
Location
Supplier

Date	Cost £	Expected life (years)	Estimated residual value	Depreciation method	Depreciation rate	Depreciation charge for the year £	Acc dep at end of the year £	Carrying amount at end of year £	Disposal proceeds £	Profit or loss on disposal £

chapter 6:
ACCRUALS AND PREPAYMENTS

chapter coverage 📖

In this chapter we consider the accounting treatment of expenses and income, in particular in the context of the accounting concept of accruals.

The topics covered are:

- ✍ The accruals concept
- ✍ Accruals of expenses
- ✍ Prepayments of expenses
- ✍ Accruals of income
- ✍ Prepayments of income

THE ACCRUALS CONCEPT

In Chapter 2 we considered the accounting concept of accruals or matching. The basic principle of the ACCRUALS CONCEPT is that the amount of income and expense that is included in the financial statements for an accounting period should be the income earned and the expenses incurred during the period rather than the cash received or paid. In this chapter we shall start to look at the practical application of this concept to the maintenance of financial records and the preparation of financial statements.

Sales and purchases

When sales are made then either the cash is received now or the sale is made on credit. Either way the sale is recorded as soon as it is made. If the sale is on credit then a receivable is set up and the sale is recorded in the sales account. Therefore even though the money has not yet been received the sale has been included in the ledger accounts.

In just the same way when an invoice is received from a credit supplier this is recorded as a purchase and a payable. Even though the money has not yet been paid to the supplier the purchase has been recorded.

Therefore our system for recording sales and purchases automatically applies the accruals concept.

Expenses

The system for recording some expenses is different. Some expenses will only be recorded in the ledger accounts when the payment for the expense is made since they are first recorded in the cash book rather than the sales or purchases day book.

For example when the rent is due it is paid and the double entry is:

    Debit   Rent account
    Credit   Bank account

The phone bill may be paid by direct debit and the double entry is:

    Debit   Phone account
    Credit   Bank account

This system means that initially the only expenses that are recorded in the ledger accounts are those that have been paid rather than those that were incurred in the period.

Therefore at the end of each accounting period each expense must be considered to ensure that the full amount of that expense that has been incurred in the period is shown as the expense rather than just the amount that has been paid.

ACCRUALS OF EXPENSES

An ACCRUAL is an amount of an expense that has been incurred during the accounting period but the business has not yet received an invoice for it and it has not yet been paid for. As such it does not appear in an expense ledger account.

The accounting treatment for an accrual of expenses is as follows:

- It must be added to the balance in the expense account to ensure that all of the expense incurred in the period is included in the statement of profit or loss

- It must be shown as a type of current liability, called an accrual, in the statement of financial position

---

Task 1

A business has paid £1,110 of phone bills during the accounting year. In the new accounting period it receives a further bill for charges of £260 which relate to the old accounting year.

This will | increase/decrease | phone expenses in the old accounting year, and it will be shown as an | asset/a liability | on the statement of financial position at the year end.

All the double entry for accounting for accruals takes place within the relevant expense account.

HOW IT WORKS

Dawn Fisher runs a business designing and selling T shirts. On 31 March 20X5 she completed her first year of trading. Her electricity account shows a debit balance of £780 but on 5 April 20X5 she receives an electricity bill for the three months to 31 March 20X5 for £410.

This must be included in her accounts for the year by increasing the electricity expense by £410 and showing a liability, an accrual, for £410 in the statement of financial position.

Step 1   We debit the electricity account with the accrual (shown as accrual carried down), adding to the expense balance.

Step 2   We bring down a credit balance on the electricity account (shown as accrual brought down) which will be listed in the statement of financial position as an accrual.

Step 3   We transfer the total expense for the period to the statement of profit or loss.

Electricity account

Date	Details	£	Date	Details	£
31 Mar	Balance b/d	780	31 Mar	SPL	1,190
31 Mar	Accrual c/d	410			
		1,190			1,190
			1 Apr	Accrual b/d	410

When the electricity bill is paid in the new accounting period it will be debited to the electricity account. This cancels out the accrual brought down, leaving the account with a zero balance in respect of the new accounting period. In other words: the expense has been accounted for in the old accounting period by setting up the accrual, so paying the bill has no impact on the profit or loss of the new accounting period.

Electricity account

Date	Details	£	Date	Details	£
20 Apr	Bank/cash	410	1 Apr	Accrual b/d	410

Task 2

A business has a debit balance of £2,600 on its phone expense account for the year ended 31 December 20X4. On 12 January 20X5 it receives a phone bill which includes £480 of call charges for the three months ended 31 December 20X4.

Show the accounting entries necessary to deal with this bill.

Phone account

	£		£

PREPAYMENTS OF EXPENSES

A PREPAYMENT is the opposite of an accrual. It is an amount of an expense that has been paid in the old accounting period but that relates to the new accounting period, not the old one. As it has already been paid it will appear as part of the balance in the expense account but it does not relate to that accounting period and therefore must be removed.

BPP
LEARNING MEDIA

The accounting treatment for a prepayment is as follows:

- It must be deducted from the balance in the expense account to ensure that only the expense incurred in the period is included in the statement of profit or loss

- It must be shown as a type of current asset, called a prepayment, in the statement of financial position

As with accruals, all the double entry for accounting for prepayments takes place within the relevant expense account.

HOW IT WORKS

Dawn paid her insurance premium of £1,200 on 30 June 20X4 in advance for the following year. The insurance account reflects this with a debit balance of £1,200 at 31 March 20X5. However, only the payment for the period from 30 June 20X4 to 31 March 20X5 (nine months) actually relates to the current accounting period. The remaining three months of the premium are an expense of the new accounting period, so they must be removed from the insurance account balance at 31 March 20X5.

The amount relating to the new period – £1,200 × 3/12 = £300 – must be excluded from her accounts for the year to 31 March 20X5 by decreasing the insurance expense by £300 and showing an asset, a prepayment, for £300 in the statement of financial position.

Step 1   We credit the insurance account with the prepayment carried down, reducing the expense balance.

Step 2   We bring down a debit balance on the insurance account (prepayment b/d), which will be listed in the statement of financial position as a prepayment.

Step 3   We transfer the total expense for the period to the statement of profit or loss.

Insurance account

Date	Details	£	Date	Details	£
31 Mar	Balance b/d	1,200	31 Mar	SPL	900
			31 Mar	Prepayment c/d	300
		1,200			1,200
1 Apr	Prepayment b/d	300			

The insurance account now shows a debit balance that will be listed as a prepayment among the current assets in the statement of financial position. This balance is part of the new period's insurance expense and therefore no further adjustments are necessary.

BPP
LEARNING MEDIA

Task 3

A business pays rent for its premises quarterly in advance. The last payment was on 1 November for the following three months for £900. The business's year end is 31 December. The balance on the rent account at 31 December is £3,200.

Make the relevant entries to account for this prepayment.

Rent account

		£			£

ACCRUALS OF INCOME

The main income of a business comprises its sales, and these are automatically accounted for on the accruals basis by recognising receivables for credit sales. However, some businesses have other sources of miscellaneous income which must also be accounted for in accordance with the accruals concept.

An ACCRUAL OF INCOME is an amount of income that is due or receivable for the accounting period but that has not been received as at the end of the period.

The accounting treatment for an accrual of income is as follows:

- It must be added to the credit balance in the income account to ensure that all of the income due in the period is included in the statement of profit or loss

- It must be shown as a type of current asset, called accrued income or income receivable, in the statement of financial position

All the double entry for accounting for accruals of income takes place within the relevant income account.

HOW IT WORKS

Dawn Fisher sells some clothes made by another business and receives a commission for the amounts that she sells. The commission received for the year to 31 March 20X5 has been £2,300 but there is a further £400 due for March commissions.

BPP LEARNING MEDIA

The accounting methods and entries are the same as for accruals and prepayments of expenses but you do need to think quite carefully about the entries as we are now dealing with income and not expenses.

The £400 income due but not received must be included in Dawn's accounts for the year by increasing the commission income by £400 and showing an asset, accrued income, for £400 in the statement of financial position.

Step 1   We credit the commission income account with the accrual of income carried down, adding to the income balance.

Step 2   We bring down a debit balance on the commission income account (accrued income b/d), which will be listed in the statement of financial position as accrued income.

Step 3   We transfer the total income for the period to the statement of profit or loss.

Commission income account

Date	Details	£	Date	Details	£
31 Mar	SPL	2,700	31 Mar	Balance b/d	2,300
			31 Mar	Accrued income c/d	400
		2,700			2,700
1 Apr	Accrued income b/d	400			

Again the correct amount is credited to the statement of profit or loss and the debit balance on the account is listed in the statement of financial position as accrued income or commission receivable (a current asset).

PREPAYMENTS OF INCOME

It is also possible for another party to prepay income to the business. A PREPAYMENT OF INCOME is miscellaneous income that has been received in the old period but which was due in the new accounting period.

The accounting treatment for a prepayment of income is as follows:

- It must be deducted from the balance in the income account to ensure that only the income due in the period is included in the statement of profit or loss

- It must be shown as a type of current liability, called prepaid income or income received in advance, in the statement of financial position

BPP
LEARNING MEDIA

HOW IT WORKS

Dawn Fisher sublets some of her premises to a local artist for a quarterly rental payable in advance of £250. The rental income account at 31 March 20X5 shows a credit balance of £1,000 but this includes £250 paid on 28 March for the following quarter.

The £250 income received in advance must be excluded from Dawn's accounts for the year by decreasing rental income by £250 and showing a liability, income received in advance, for £250 in the statement of financial position.

Step 1   We debit the rental income account with the prepayment of income carried down, reducing the income balance.

Step 2   We bring down a credit balance on the rental income account (prepaid income b/d), which will be listed in the statement of financial position as income received in advance.

Step 3   We transfer the total income for the period to the statement of profit or loss.

Rental income account

Date	Details	£	Date	Details	£
31 Mar	SPL	750	31 Mar	Balance b/d	1,000
31 Mar	Prepaid income c/d	250			
		1,000			1,000
			1 Apr	Prepaid income b/d	250

Again the income appearing in the statement of profit or loss is the correct amount of £750 and a credit balance of £250, income received in advance, is listed as a current liability in the statement of financial position.

Task 4

How is accrued income accounted for in the statement of financial position?

	✓
Asset	
Liability	

CHAPTER OVERVIEW

- Accounts should be prepared according to the accruals concept which means that the income and expenses that are recognised should be those that have been earned or incurred in the period, not just the amounts of cash that have been received or paid

- By setting up control accounts for sales and purchases on credit these sales and purchases are automatically recorded according to the accruals concept – the sale and purchase is recognised when it is made not when the cash is received or paid

- Expenses are however treated differently – some expenses will only be recorded in the expense ledger account when they are actually paid, therefore at the end of each accounting year each expense account must be considered carefully to ensure that the balance represents the full amount of that expense that has been incurred in the period

- An accrual is an amount of expense that has been incurred but has not yet been invoiced for or paid and is therefore not yet recorded in the expense ledger account – this accrual must be added to the expense balance and shown in the statement of financial position as a liability, an accrual

- A prepayment is the opposite of an accrual – it is an amount of expense that has been paid and therefore appears in the ledger account but it relates to the following accounting period. This must be removed from the ledger account balance and is shown in the statement of financial position as a form of asset, a prepayment

- Many businesses will have sources of miscellaneous income – these can also be either accrued or prepaid

- An accrual of income is an amount that is due for the period but has not been received – this must be added to the income account balance and included in the statement of financial position as a form of asset, called accrued income or income receivable

- A prepayment of income is where income has been received but it actually relates to the following accounting period – this must be deducted from the income account balance and shown in the statement of financial position as a liability, income received in advance

Keywords

Accruals concept – fundamental accounting concept that states that income and expenses shown in the statement of profit or loss should be those that were earned or incurred during the period rather than simply the cash received or paid

Accrual – an amount of expense that has been incurred during the period but that has not yet been invoiced for or paid

Prepayment – an amount of expense that has been paid for but that relates to the following accounting period

Accrual of income – an amount of income that is due for the period but that has not yet been received

Prepayment of income – an amount of income that has been received but that relates to the following accounting period

TEST YOUR LEARNING

Test 1

(a) Rent paid in advance for the following accounting period would appear as | an accrual/a prepayment | in the statement of financial position.

(b) Motor expenses owing to the local garage would appear as | an accrual /a prepayment | in the statement of financial position.

Test 2

State what effect each of the following would have in the statement of profit or loss and the statement of financial position of a business with an accounting year end of 31 March 20XX:

(a) The balance on the heat and light expense account of £670 does not include the latest bill which shows £200 of heat and light expenses for the first three months of 20XX.

In the statement of profit or loss the heat and light expense would be £ [   ] . In the statement of financial position there would be | an accrual/a prepayment | for £ [   ] .

(b) The rental income account balance of £380 includes £40 of rent received for April 20XX.

In the statement of profit or loss the rental income would be £ [   ] . In the statement of financial position there would be | an accrual of income/a prepayment of income | for £ [   ] .

(c) The insurance account balance of £1,400 includes £300 for insurance for April to June 20XX.

In the statement of profit or loss the insurance expense would be £ [   ] .

In the statement of financial position there would be | an accrual/a prepayment | for £ [   ] .

(d) The commissions income account balance of £180 does not include £20 of commission due for March 20XX.

In the statement of profit or loss commissions income would be £ [   ] . In the statement of financial position there would be | an accrual of income/a prepayment of income | for £ [   ] .

Test 3

A business has an accounting year end of 30 June 20XX. On that date the motor expenses account shows a balance of £845. This includes £150 of road fund licence for the year from 1 January 20XX.

Show the accounting entries required for this in the motor expenses account.

Motor expenses account

		£			£

Test 4

A business has an accounting year end of 31 March 20XX. At that date the balance on the electricity account is £470. On 7 April 20XX a further electricity bill is received for January to March 20XX totalling £180. This bill is then paid on 25 April 20XX.

Show the accounting entries in the electricity account that are required to show the correct picture at the year end.

Electricity account

		£			£

chapter 7:
INVENTORY

INTRODUCTION TO INVENTORY

Businesses make a great many purchases of items for resale or for use in manufacture and administration. There is nearly always a timing difference between when the items are purchased and when they are used, and during that time they are held 'in inventory' (IAS) or 'in stock' (UK GAAP).

At a period end therefore the holding of inventory presents the accountant with a problem connected yet again with the **accruals** concept. When items are purchased either for cash or on credit the debit entry is always made to the purchases account, never to an 'inventory' or 'stock' account. Unless an adjustment is made to the purchases account, because of the timing difference it will include the cost not only of items that have been bought and used in the period but also of items that the business still holds at the period end. The income connected with the items which are in inventory at the period end will be earned in the new period.

At the end of each accounting period the business's inventory is:

- Physically counted

- Valued, then

- Adjusted in the ledger accounts so there is a statement of financial position asset and a credit to cost of sales in the statement of profit or loss

We shall follow each step through in turn.

RECORDING AND COUNTING ITEMS OF INVENTORY

For each item purchased there will be a stores record which shows the quantity purchased each time a delivery arrives, the quantity issued to sell or to process further in the factory, and the quantity on hand at any point in time. By this means the business tries to control and look after its key asset.

HOW IT WORKS

Dawn Fisher buys a variety of different coloured T shirts, in different sizes, to decorate. The stores record, in units, for March 20X5 for the extra small white T shirts is given below:

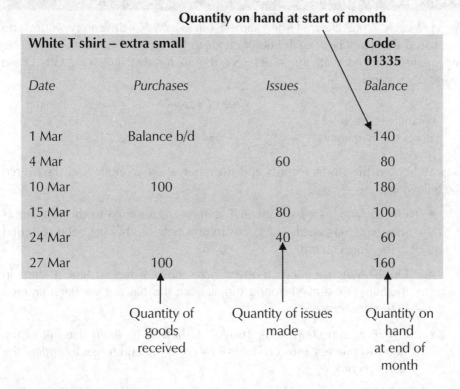

Quantity on hand at start of month

White T shirt – extra small			Code 01335
Date	Purchases	Issues	Balance
1 Mar	Balance b/d		140
4 Mar		60	80
10 Mar	100		180
15 Mar		80	100
24 Mar		40	60
27 Mar	100		160

Quantity of goods received   Quantity of issues made   Quantity on hand at end of month

Physical count

At the end of the accounting period each item of inventory is physically counted and listed. The quantity counted is then compared to the stores records. If there is a discrepancy between the actual quantity of inventory counted and the balance on the stores record then this must be investigated. The difference will normally be due to errors in the recording of purchases or issues of the item. However, if there are fewer items than the records show then care should be taken to identify whether items have been stolen.

This process is known as the PHYSICAL INVENTORY COUNT and often takes place at other times of the year as well as at the year end in order to keep control over the business's inventory. However, the year end inventory count is the most important as this is the one which will provide the figure for inventory that will appear in the financial statements.

CLOSING INVENTORY RECONCILIATION

The physical quantity of each item must be checked to the stores record and any discrepancies investigated. This is done in the form of an INVENTORY RECONCILIATION.

HOW IT WORKS

At 31 March 20X5 Dawn Fisher carried out a physical inventory count and compared the quantity of each line of goods to the stores records. In most cases the quantity agreed with the stores records but for two lines of goods Dawn found discrepancies.

	Green T – large	Blue T – medium
Quantity counted	48	150
Stores record quantity	54	126

Dawn checked the stores records and documentation carefully and discovered the following:

- On 26 March six large green T shirts were returned to the supplier as they were damaged. The goods returns note has not yet been recorded in the stores record

- On 30 March a goods received note showed that 40 blue T shirts in medium size arrived from a supplier but this has not yet been entered in the stores record

- On 28 March Dawn took 16 blue T shirts in medium size out of the stores to process a rush order from a customer and forgot to update the stores record

Using these facts Dawn now prepares her inventory reconciliation.

Inventory reconciliation – 31 March 20X5

Green T – large	Quantity
Stores record	54
Less returned to supplier 26 March	(6)
Counted 31 March	48

Blue T – medium	Quantity
Stores record	126
Add goods received note 30 March	40
Less items issued for sale 28 March	(16)
Counted 31 March	150

VALUING INVENTORY

Dawn can now use her physical count quantities to prepare her closing inventory valuation for each line of goods.

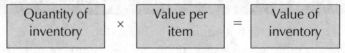

Quantity of inventory × Value per item = Value of inventory

BPP LEARNING MEDIA

Lower of cost and NRV rule

The rules for valuing inventory come from IAS 2. The basic rule for valuation is:

Inventory should be valued at the lower of COST and NET REALISABLE VALUE.

Before we look at what is included in these two figures we will consider the purpose of this rule.

It is based upon the accounting concept of **prudence**, which we saw in Chapter 2. The normal situation is that an item will be purchased for say £30 and then resold for £40. In this case the inventory will be valued at cost of £30. However, suppose the item could only be sold for £25. If we valued it at £30 we would be overstating its value as an asset. The prudence concept does not allow this so the item must be valued at its selling price of £25.

So what are cost and net realisable value?

- IAS 2 states that cost comprises 'all costs of purchase, costs of conversion and other costs incurred in bringing the items to their present location and condition'

- NET REALISABLE VALUE is the expected selling price of the inventory, less any further costs to be incurred such as selling or distribution costs. IAS 2 defines it as 'the estimated selling price in the ordinary course of business less the estimated costs of completion and the estimated costs necessary to make the sale'

Task 1

A product that a business sells costs £13.80 to buy. Due to a fall in demand for this product it will only sell for £14.00 and in order to sell at this price it must be delivered to the customer at a cost of 50p per unit.

At what value should inventory of this product be included in the financial statements?

£ [＿＿＿＿＿＿＿]

HOW IT WORKS

A small business has three lines of inventory A, B and C. The total cost and total net realisable value (NRV) of each line is given below:

	Cost	NRV
	£	£
A	1,250	2,000
B	1,400	1,200
C	1,100	1,900
	3,750	5,100

Although the total cost of £3,750 is lower than the total net realisable value of £5,100 this is not the value of the business's closing inventory. The cost and net realisable value must be compared for each individual line of inventory as follows:

	Cost	NRV	Lower = Inventory value
	£	£	£
A	1,250	2,000	1,250
B	1,400	1,200	1,200
C	1,100	1,900	1,100
	3,750	5,100	3,550

The inventory should be valued at £3,550 which is the total of the lower of cost and net realisable value for each line.

METHODS OF DETERMINING COST

Before they can apply the cost/NRV rule, businesses are often faced with the problem of determining the actual cost price of the items held. If there are deliveries and issues of an item on a regular basis then it will be difficult (if not impossible) to determine precisely which items have been sold and which remain as the closing inventory. If the prices at which each batch of the item was purchased differ then it becomes important that we know which purchases remain in inventory at the end of the accounting period.

The time and effort involved in determining exactly which item has been sold and exactly which remains in inventory will usually not be worthwhile for a business. Therefore the cost of inventory will be determined by using one of a number of assumptions as follows:

- **FIFO (FIRST IN FIRST OUT)** we assume that the items issued are the earliest purchases, so the inventory on hand comprise the most recent purchases

- **LIFO (LAST IN FIRST OUT)** we assume that the items issued are the most recent purchases, so the items in inventory are the earliest purchases. Some businesses will use this method for day-to-day stock control in practice but IAS 2 forbids it

- **AVCO (WEIGHTED AVERAGE COST)** after each new purchase a weighted average cost for the items held is calculated – this is the total cost of the items held divided by the number of units held – the inventory is valued at this weighted average at the end of the period

HOW IT WORKS

Dawn Fisher's stores record for extra small white T shirts for March is shown below.

White T shirt – extra small   **Code 01335**

Date	Purchases	Issues	Balance
1 Mar	Balance b/d		140
15 Mar		80	60
27 Mar	100		160
28 Mar		40	120

The 140 items held on 1 March were all purchased at £7 per unit, and the purchase on 27 March was at £8 per unit.

The value of the 120 units remaining in inventory at the end of the month will be calculated on the FIFO, LIFO and AVCO basis.

FIFO – First in first out

Date	Purchases units	Cost/ unit £	Issues units	Cost/ unit £	Total units	Cost/ units £	Total cost £
1 Mar (b/d)					140	7.00	980.00
15 Mar			(80)		(80)	7.00	(560.00)
27 Mar	100	8.00			100	8.00	800.00
28 Mar			(40)		(40)	7.00	(280.00)
					120		940.00

LIFO – Last in first out

Date	Purchases units	Cost/ unit £	Issues units	Cost/ unit £	Total units	Cost/ units £	Total cost £
1 Mar (b/d)					140	7.00	980.00
15 Mar			(80)		(80)	7.00	(560.00)
27 Mar	100	8.00			100	8.00	800.00
28 Mar			(40)	8.00	(40)	8.00	(320.00)
					120		900.00

AVCO – Weighted average cost

Date	Purchases quantity	Cost per unit £	Issues units	Cost per unit £	Balance Units	Balance £
1 Mar Bal b/d	140	7.00		7.00	140	980.00
15 Mar			(80)	7.00	(80)	(560.00)
27 Mar	100	8.00		8.00	100	800.00
	Av. cost	1,220/160		7.625	160	1,220.00
28 Mar			(40)	7.625	(40)	(305.00)
					120	915.00

As you can see the values of the inventory under the different methods vary:

	£
FIFO	940.00
LIFO	900.00
AVCO	915.00

Task 2

A business buys 100 units of a product for £3.50 per unit on 1 May. A further 100 units are purchased on 20 May for £4.00 per unit. The sales for the month were 70 units on 12 May and 80 units on 30 May.

Determine the value of the closing inventory using the FIFO method.

£ [   ]

LEDGER ACCOUNTING FOR INVENTORY

Whenever goods are purchased they must be debited to a purchases account, **never** to an inventory account. The inventory account is only used at the end of the accounting period in order to record the closing inventory of the business.

HOW IT WORKS

Dawn Fisher has counted and valued all of her inventory at her year end 31 March 20X5 and it totals £6,450.

This figure is entered into the ledger accounts by a debit and a credit entry to two different inventory accounts:

Debit Inventory account – statement of financial position
Credit Inventory account – statement of profit or loss

Inventory account – statement of financial position

	£		£
31 Mar 20X5	6,450		

Inventory account – statement of profit or loss

	£		£
		31 Mar 20X5	6,450

The inventory – statement of financial position account balance, a debit balance, is the closing inventory asset that will be listed in the statement of financial position as a current asset.

The inventory – statement of profit or loss balance is cleared out to the statement of profit or loss at the end of the year, to be shown eventually as a deduction from purchases to give the cost of sales figure.

Inventory account – statement of profit or loss

	£		£
31 Mar 20X5 SPL	6,450	31 Mar 20X5	6,450

Dawn's purchases account at the end of the year shows a debit balance of £76,850. This is also cleared to the statement of profit or loss for the year. We deduct the inventory account – statement of profit or loss balance to arrive at the figure for cost of sales:

	£
Cost of sales as at 31 March 20X5:	
Purchases	76,850
Less closing inventory	(6,450)
	70,400

The only inventory balance that remains in Dawn's books now is that on the inventory – statement of financial position account. This remains in her ledger accounts as the opening inventory balance without any further entries to it until the end of the following accounting period, 31 March 20X6. At this date the closing inventory is valued at £7,200 and the purchases for the year were £80,900.

As this is Dawn's second year we have both opening and closing inventory.

Step 1 At 31 March 20X6, clear the balance on the inventory account (which is the opening inventory), to the statement of profit or loss.

Inventory account – statement of financial position

	£		£
1 Apr 20X5 Bal b/d Opening inventory	6,450	31 Mar 20X6 SPL	6,450

Step 2 Enter the closing inventory valuation at 31 March 20X6 into the two inventory accounts:

Inventory account – statement of financial position

	£		£
		31 Mar 20X6 SPL	6,450
1 Apr 20X5 Bal b/d Opening inventory	6,450		
31 Mar 20X6 Closing inventory	7,200		

Inventory account – statement of profit or loss

	£		£
		31 Mar 20X6 Closing inventory	7,200

Step 3 Clear the account for inventory – statement of profit or loss to the statement of profit or loss as the closing inventory:

Inventory account – statement of profit or loss

	£		£
31 Mar 20X6 SPL	7,200	31 Mar 20X6 Closing inventory	7,200

Step 4 Calculate the cost of sales in the statement of profit or loss for the year ended 31 March 20X6:

	£
Cost of sales as at 31 March 20X6:	
Opening inventory	6,450
Purchases	80,900
	87,350
Less closing inventory	(7,200)
	80,150

Journal entry for recording closing inventory

The journal entry with narrative for recording the closing inventory for Dawn Fisher would be as follows:

Account name	Debit £	Credit £
Inventory account – statement of financial position	7,200	
Inventory account – statement of profit or loss		7,200

Being inventory held at 31 March 20X6

To summarise:

Statement of profit or loss

- Debit with opening inventory
- Credit with closing inventory

Statement of financial position

- Debit with closing inventory as a current asset

This may seem complicated now but when we start dealing with the extended trial balance it will become second nature!

Task 3

When goods are purchased the cost should be debited to which ledger account:

	✓
Inventory	
Purchases	

CHAPTER OVERVIEW

- When goods are purchased they are always debited to a purchases account and never to an inventory account

- At the end of the year, and often at other times during the year, the inventory must be counted and the quantity of each item listed – this is then compared to the stores record of the amount of that item that should exist – an inventory reconciliation will be carried out

- Once the quantity of each item of inventory is known then it must be valued – both SSAP 9 and IAS 2 state that each line of inventory should be valued at the lower of cost and net realisable value (NRV)

- In order to determine the cost of inventory a method has to be chosen – the most common methods are FIFO, LIFO (not permitted under IAS 2) and AVCO (weighted average cost)

- When the closing inventory has been valued it must be included in the final accounts as a current asset in the statement of financial position and as a deduction from purchases to give cost of sales in the statement of profit or loss

- Opening inventory for a period is included as an expense in the statement of profit or loss, being added to the purchases figure in the cost of sales calculation

Keywords

Inventory count – the regular and year end process of counting each line of inventory and comparing the quantity to the quantity that should exist according to the stores records

Closing inventory reconciliation – comparison of inventory record quantity to quantity actually counted

Cost – the cost for inventory is the cost of getting the inventory to its current position which will include delivery costs

Net realisable value (NRV) – the expected selling price of the item less any further costs to be incurred such as selling or distribution expenses

FIFO – first in first out – method of inventory valuation that assumes that items issued are the earliest purchases so closing inventory contains the most recent purchases

LIFO – last in first out – method of inventory valuation that assumes that the items issued are the most recent purchases so closing inventory contains the earliest purchases

AVCO – weighted average cost – method of inventory valuation that operates by calculating a weighted average cost for the inventory after each new purchase

TEST YOUR LEARNING

Test 1

A business has 120 units of an item at the year end which cost £25.80 plus delivery charges of £1.00 per unit. This item can be sold for £28.00 per unit but must be delivered to the customer at a further cost of £1.10 per unit.

(a) The cost of each item is £ [   ] and the net realisable value of each item is £ [   ].

(b) At what value would these 120 units appear in the statement of financial position?

£ [   ]

chapter 8:
IRRECOVERABLE DEBTS AND DOUBTFUL DEBTS

chapter coverage 📖

In this chapter we consider the receivables balance at the end of the accounting year and any adjustments that are required.

The topics covered are:

✍ Introduction to irrecoverable debts

✍ Accounting for irrecoverable debts

✍ Accounting for irrecoverable debts recovered

✍ Introduction to doubtful debts

✍ Accounting for doubtful debts

✍ Specific and general allowances for doubtful debts

✍ Adjusting the allowance for doubtful debts

INTRODUCTION TO IRRECOVERABLE DEBTS

When a sale is made on credit it is recognised immediately in the accounting records by recording it as a sale and setting up a receivable for the amount due – this is in accordance with the **accruals** concept. We expect the debt to be honoured and the amount paid by the customer. However, it is possible that some debts may never be paid so, in line with the **prudence** concept and to avoid any overstatement of assets, any debts that are unlikely to be paid should not be shown as an asset in the statement of financial position.

An IRRECOVERABLE DEBT is one that the business believes will never be paid (you may sometimes hear it being referred to as a 'bad debt').

ACCOUNTING FOR IRRECOVERABLE DEBTS

If a debt is not going to be recovered then it should be removed from the business's accounts and it should not be shown as a receivable in the statement of financial position. This is known as writing off the irrecoverable debt.

The double entry for this is:

Debit   Irrecoverable debts expense account
Credit   Sales ledger control account

This will remove the debt from the receivables balance and create an expense – irrecoverable debts expense – in the statement of profit or loss.

The customer's individual account in the sales ledger must also have the debt removed from it by a credit entry here as well.

HOW IT WORKS

The balance on Dawn Fisher's sales ledger control account at the year end date of 31 March 20X5 is £10,857. She is however very concerned about an amount of £337 owing from K Whistler. The last money received from this customer was in September 20X4 and Dawn's latest letter has been returned unopened with a scribbled comment on the envelope 'K Whistler not known at this address'. Dawn has now decided to accept that the debt will never be paid and is to write it off as irrecoverable.

Irrecoverable debts expense account

Date	Details	£	Date	Details	£
31 Mar	Sales ledger control	337			

Sales ledger control account

Date	Details	£	Date	Details	£
31 Mar	Balance b/d	10,857	31 Mar	Irrecoverable debts expense	337
			31 Mar	Balance c/d	10,520
		10,857			10,857
1 Apr	Balance b/d	10,520			

The sales ledger control account now shows the amended balance of £10,520 after having removed K Whistler's debt. The irrecoverable debts expense account has a debit balance of £337 which is an expense of the business, one of the risks of making sales on credit, and as such will be charged in the statement of profit or loss as an expense.

In the sales ledger K Whistler's account must also be credited with the amount of this irrecoverable debt to remove it from these records as well:

K Whistler

Date	Details	£	Date	Details	£
31 Mar	Balance b/d	337	31 Mar	Irrecoverable debt written off	337

Task 1

A business has receivables at the year end of £26,478. Of these it is felt that £976 should be written off as irrecoverable.

What is the journal entry, including narrative, for the write-off of these irrecoverable debts?

Account name	Debit £	Credit £

ACCOUNTING FOR IRRECOVERABLE DEBTS RECOVERED

Occasionally a debt will be settled by a customer after it has been written off by the business as irrecoverable.

The double entry for this requires the expense of the write-off to be removed from the irrecoverable debts account – as it has already been written off there is no adjustment to the sales ledger control account:

Debit   Bank/cash account
Credit   Irrecoverable debts expense account

Task 2

A business has written off a debt for £1,000 from one of its customers and then three months later the amount is received.

Prepare the journal entry, including narrative, to record the recovery.

Account name	Debit £	Credit £

INTRODUCTION TO DOUBTFUL DEBTS

We have seen that an irrecoverable debt is one that we are fairly sure will never be recovered. There may also be other debts that we are concerned about but that we are not yet ready to write off as irrecoverable. Our concern may arise from a customer querying an amount or not responding to initial requests for payment of an overdue debt.

These debts over which there is some concern are known as DOUBTFUL DEBTS.

There is also another scenario with customers owing money. A business may not necessarily be able to pinpoint specific debts that are doubtful but the sales ledger clerk may know from experience that, on average, a certain percentage of debts turn out to be doubtful. In this case the percentage can be applied to the total receivables figure to give an indication of the amount of doubtful debts.

ACCOUNTING FOR DOUBTFUL DEBTS

According to the **prudence** concept if there is uncertainty as to the recoverability of debts then there is a possibility that an asset – receivables – will be overstated in the statement of financial position. While we need to include the most cautious figure for assets in the statement of financial position, we do not want to remove these debts from the sales ledger control account since they may well yet be recovered, unlike an irrecoverable debt. Consequently, we set up an ALLOWANCE FOR DOUBTFUL DEBTS.

An allowance is a ledger account with a credit balance which is deducted (or 'netted off') against an asset ledger account when the statement of financial position is prepared. The allowance for doubtful debts account is similar therefore to the accumulated depreciation account. On the statement of financial position this is presented as a depreciation balance that is deducted from the non-current assets at cost balance in order to arrive at their carrying amount.

In a similar way the allowance for doubtful debts is a credit balance which is deducted from the sales ledger control account balance to show the net figure for receivables that are recoverable in the statement of financial position. It is a less permanent way of achieving the prudent figure for receivables than writing the debt out of the sales ledger control account as an irrecoverable debt.

Double entry to set up an allowance for doubtful debts

The double entry to set up an allowance for doubtful debts is:

Debit   Allowance for doubtful debts adjustment account
Credit   Allowance for doubtful debts account

The ALLOWANCE FOR DOUBTFUL DEBTS ADJUSTMENT ACCOUNT is an expense account that will have a debit balance when an allowance is first set up.

SPECIFIC AND GENERAL ALLOWANCES FOR DOUBTFUL DEBTS

We have seen that there are potentially two types of doubtful debt – the specific debts that can be pinpointed as doubtful and the more general percentage approach.

This means that a business could have a policy of having two elements to its allowance for doubtful debts:

- A SPECIFIC ALLOWANCE
- A GENERAL ALLOWANCE

HOW IT WORKS

Dawn Fisher's balance on her sales ledger control account at 31 March 20X5 after writing off the irrecoverable debt from K Whistler is £10,520.

When Dawn considers these debts in detail she decides that she is concerned about the recoverability of one debt for £320. She has also been advised by friends in business that she is likely to have problems on average with about 2% of her receivables.

Therefore Dawn's policy is to set up an allowance for doubtful debts made up of two elements:

- A specific allowance for £320
- A general allowance of 2% of the remaining balance of receivables

Step 1 Calculate the total amount of the allowance. Before applying a percentage to the sales ledger control account total to calculate a general allowance you should always deduct:

- Any irrecoverable debts that are to be written off
- Any debts against which a specific allowance is to be made

	£
Sales ledger control account balance after writing off irrecoverable debts	10,520
Specific allowance	(320)
	10,200
General allowance 2% × £10,200	204
Specific allowance	320
Amount of allowance to be set up	524

Step 2 Enter the allowance into the ledger accounts.

Allowance for doubtful debts adjustment account

Date	Details	£	Date	Details	£
31 Mar	Allowance for doubtful debts	524	31 Mar	SPL	524
		524			524

Allowance for doubtful debts

Date	Details	£	Date	Details	£
			31 Mar	Allowance for doubtful debts adjustment	524

Step 3 Close off the balance on the allowance for doubtful debts adjustment account of £524 to the statement of profit or loss as an expense.

Step 4 When Dawn produces her statement of financial position the sales ledger control account balance will have the allowance deducted from it to show the figure for receivables that are truly recoverable:

	£
Sales ledger control account	10,520
Less allowance for doubtful debts account	(524)
Receivables figure in the statement of financial position	9,996

Task 3

A business has a sales ledger control account balance of £21,680. One debt of £680 is to be written off as irrecoverable and an allowance of 3% is to be made against the remainder.

Prepare the journal entries, including narrative, to record the irrecoverable debt and the allowance being set up.

Account name	Debit £	Credit £

ADJUSTING THE ALLOWANCE FOR DOUBTFUL DEBTS

In subsequent years the balance on the allowance for doubtful debts account will remain in the ledger accounts as it is a statement of financial position account, but it may require increasing or decreasing each year.

To increase the allowance for doubtful debts the double entry is:

Debit   Allowance for doubtful debts adjustment account
Credit   Allowance for doubtful debts account

- With the amount of the increase required

To decrease the allowance for doubtful debts the double entry is:

Debit   Allowance for doubtful debts account
Credit   Allowance for doubtful debts adjustment account

- With the amount of the decrease required

HOW IT WORKS

A business has a policy of providing against 4% of its receivables at the year end. Its sales ledger control account balance at 31 December 20X6, the end of its first year of trading, was £24,000 after writing off irrecoverable debts of £200. At the end of 20X7 and 20X8 the balances were £30,000 and £26,000 again after writing off irrecoverable debts of £400 and £300 respectively.

Step 1 Calculate the allowances required at the end of each year:

20X6 £24,000 × 4%   = £960

20X7 £30,000 × 4%   = £1,200

20X8 £26,000 × 4%   = £1,040

Step 2 Set up the allowance for doubtful debts at 31 December 20X6.

Allowance for doubtful debts adjustment account

Date 20X6	Details	£	Date 20X6	Details	£
31 Dec	Allowance for doubtful debts	960	31 Dec	Statement of profit or loss	960
		960			960

Allowance for doubtful debts account

Date 20X6	Details	£	Date 20X6	Details	£
31 Dec			31 Dec	Allowance for doubtful debts adjustment	960
	Balance c/d	960	20X7		
			1 Jan	Balance b/d	960

The allowance has been set up by charging the whole amount to the allowance for doubtful debts adjustment account. This is then taken to the statement of profit or loss so no balance remains on that account. In contrast the allowance for doubtful debts is a statement of financial position account so it remains as the opening balance for 20X7.

Step 3 Increase allowance by (£1,200 – £960) = £240 to £1,200 at 31 December 20X7.

Allowance for doubtful debts adjustment account

Date 20X7	Details	£	Date 20X7	Details	£
31 Dec	Allowance for doubtful debts	240	31 Dec	Statement of profit or loss	240
		240			240

Allowance for doubtful debts account

Date	Details	£	Date	Details	£
20X6			20X6		
31 Dec	Balance c/d	960	31 Dec	Allowance for doubtful debts adjustment	960
20X7			20X7		
31 Dec	Balance c/d	1,200	1 Jan	Balance b/d	960
			31 Dec	Allowance for doubtful debts adjustment	240
		1,200			1,200
			20X8		
			1 Jan	Balance b/d	1,200

The allowance for doubtful debts adjustment account has only been charged with the amount that is necessary to bring the balance on the allowance up to this year's required amount of £1,200 – in this case £240.

Step 4 Decrease allowance by (£1,200 – £1,040) = £160 to £1,040 as at 31 December 20X8.

Allowance for doubtful debts adjustment account

Date	Details	£	Date	Details	£
20X8			20X8		
31 Dec	Statement of profit or loss	160	31 Dec	Allowance for doubtful debts	160
		160			300

Allowance for doubtful debts account

Date	Details	£	Date	Details	£
20X6			20X6		
31 Dec	Balance c/d	960	31 Dec	Allowance for doubtful debts adjustment	960
20X7			20X7		
31 Dec	Balance c/d	1,200	1 Jan	Balance b/d	960
			31 Dec	Allowance for doubtful debts adjustment	240
		1,200			1,200
20X8			20X8		
31 Dec	Allowance for doubtful debts adjustment	160	1 Jan	Balance b/d	1,200
31 Dec	Balance c/d	1,040			
		1,200			1,200
			20X9		
			1 Jan	Balance b/d	1,040

In this case the allowance had to be reduced by £160 so the allowance for doubtful debts adjustment account was credited and the allowance account debited in order to bring the allowance account balance down to the amount required.

At each year end in the statement of financial position the receivables would appear as follows:

	20X6 £	20X7 £	20X8 £
Sales ledger control account	24,000	30,000	26,000
Less allowance for doubtful debts	960	1,200	1,040
Receivables	23,040	28,800	24,960

Task 4

On 31 December 20X7 a business had a balance on its allowance for doubtful debts account of £1,500. At the year end of 31 December 20X8 its sales ledger control account balance was £60,000. On consideration of these debts it was decided that £2,400 were to be written off as irrecoverable debts and that an allowance of 1% was to be made against the remainder.

Prepare the journal entries, including narrative, to record the irrecoverable debt and the adjustment to the allowance.

Account name	Debit £	Credit £

Task 5

What is the double entry when the allowance for doubtful debts is to be **decreased**?

Account name	Debit £	Credit £
Allowance for doubtful debts (SFP)		
Allowance for doubtful debts adj (IS)		

Task 6

Setting up an allowance for doubtful debts is an example of which accounting concept?

Going concern/accruals/prudence/materiality/consistency.

CHAPTER OVERVIEW

- The accruals concept requires that sales on credit are recognised as soon as they are made rather than waiting until the cash is received from the customer – the prudence concept however requires that if money from a customer is unlikely to be received then it should not appear as an asset in the statement of financial position

- Any debts that are not going to be recovered should be written off as irrecoverable debts by debiting the irrecoverable debts expense account and crediting the sales ledger control account – the customer's individual account in the subsidiary sales ledger must also be credited with the amount of the irrecoverable debt

- If a customer eventually pays a debt that has already been written off as an irrecoverable debt then the bank/cash account is debited with the receipt and the irrecoverable debts expense account is credited

- A doubtful debt is one where there is concern about its recoverability – these are dealt with in the accounting records by setting up an allowance for doubtful debts

- In some cases the allowance will be against specific debts and in other cases a general allowance will be required at a percentage of the sales ledger control account balance less the specific allowance

- Once the allowance for doubtful debts has initially been set up then each year the balance must be increased or decreased to the amount that is required – this is done by debiting or crediting the allowance for doubtful debts adjustment account by the amount of the increase or decrease required

Keywords

Irrecoverable debt – a debt that it is believed will not be paid

Irrecoverable debts expense account – the expense account used to record the irrecoverable debts that are written off – the balance appears as an expense in the statement of profit or loss

Doubtful debts – amounts over which there is some doubt as to their recoverability

Allowance for doubtful debts – an amount that will be deducted from the sales ledger control account balance in the statement of financial position to reduce the balance for receivables to the prudent amount

Allowance for doubtful debts adjustment account – the account used to record the setting up and then adjustment of the allowance for doubtful debts – the balance appears initially as an expense in the statement of profit or loss), though in subsequent periods it may appear as income (when the allowance is reduced)

Specific allowance – an allowance against particular debts that are recognised as doubtful

General allowance – an allowance set up as a percentage of the receivables balance to reflect the fact that on average a certain percentage of debts will be doubtful

BPP
LEARNING MEDIA

TEST YOUR LEARNING

Test 1

A business has receivables at 30 April 20XX of £25,673. Of these it was decided that two debts were never going to be recovered, £157 from H Taylor and £288 from C Phelps. These are to be written off as irrecoverable.

Write up the general ledger and sales ledger accounts necessary to record these irrecoverable debts.

General ledger

Sales ledger control account

	£		£

Irrecoverable debts expense account

	£		£

Sales ledger

H Taylor

	£		£

C Phelps

	£		£

Test 2

In 20X7 a business had written off an irrecoverable debt from a customer of £250. During 20X8 this amount was unexpectedly received from the customer.

Write up the general ledger accounts in full to reflect this receipt.

Bank account

	£		£

Irrecoverable debts expense account

	£		£

Test 3

At the end of the first year of trading a business has a sales ledger control account balance of £11,650. Of these it is decided that one debt of £350 is to be written off as irrecoverable. An allowance for doubtful debts is to be made against a further debt of £200 and a general allowance is required of 2% of the remainder.

(a) Calculate the amount of the allowance for doubtful debts that is required at the year end.

£ [   ]

(b) Write up the irrecoverable debts expense account, sales ledger control account, allowance for doubtful debts adjustment account and allowance for doubtful debts account at the year end to reflect the position.

Irrecoverable debts expense account

	£		£

Sales ledger control account

	£		£

Allowance for doubtful debts adjustment account

	£		£

Allowance for doubtful debts account

	£		£

Test 4

On 1 January 20X7 there is a balance on a business's allowance for doubtful debts account of £1,460. At 31 December 20X7 the balance on the sales ledger control account is £42,570. Of this it is decided that £370 should be written off as an irrecoverable debt and an allowance for doubtful debts of 4% is required against the remainder.

At 31 December 20X8 the sales ledger control account total was £38,400 of which £400 is to be written off as an irrecoverable debt. An allowance for doubtful debts of 4% of the remainder is required.

Write up the irrecoverable debts expense account, the allowance for doubtful debts adjustment account and the allowance for doubtful debts account for 20X7 and 20X8.

Irrecoverable debts expense account

	£		£

Allowance for doubtful debts adjustment account

	£		£

Allowance for doubtful debts account

	£		£

chapter 9:
BANK RECONCILIATIONS

chapter coverage 📖

The cash book is one of the main books of prime entry and it is vital for any business to ensure control over its cash in hand and held at the bank. A key means of control is through the bank reconciliation process.

The topics covered are:

✍ Purpose of bank reconciliations

✍ Checking the bank statement to the cash book

✍ Bank reconciliation statement

PURPOSE OF BANK RECONCILIATIONS

The bank reconciliation process, which is covered in detail for Level 2 in Control accounts, journals and the banking system involves checking transactions recorded in the bank account columns in the business's cash book to the bank statement issued by the business's bank.

In theory the balance on the cash book and on the bank statement should be the same, but in practice timing differences mean that they very rarely are.

Carrying out the bank reconciliation process has three purposes:

- To help **identify errors**:
    - Made by the business in writing up its cash book
    - Made by the bank in maintaining the business's bank account

- To help **identify omissions**:
    - From the cash book, such as bank charges and dishonoured cheques processed by the bank

    - From the bank statement, such as cheques that have been sent out to suppliers but have not yet been presented for payment

- To **verify the accuracy** of the balance for cash at bank as presented in financial statements at the end of the accounting period. Since the bank is a separate entity from the business, identifying and explaining the differences between the bank statement balance and the cash book balance means that a form of external verification has taken place.

CHECKING THE BANK STATEMENT TO THE CASH BOOK

When checking the bank statement to the cash book it should always be borne in mind that the bank statement and the cash book are mirror images of each other:

- A **debit entry in the cash book** – a receipt of money – will appear as a **credit on the bank statement**.

- A **credit entry in the cash book** – a payment of money – will appear as a **debit on the bank statement**.

A bank account which is 'in credit' according to the bank will have a debit balance on its cash book. A bank account which is 'overdrawn' according to the bank has a credit balance on the cash book – it is a liability, known as an overdraft, not an asset.

A bank statement for Anna Murphy is set out below as an example:

GREEN BANK

19 Market Square, Hentage, FR9 9PO

STATEMENT

Account Name:

Anna Murphy

Account No: 73-23-23 75487325

Date	Details	DEBITS (Payments)	CREDITS (Receipts)	Balance
		£	£	£
21/09	Balance b/d			10,000.00 CR
22/09	BGC		2,400.00	
	Bank charges	15.00		
	BACS – salaries	1,200.00		
	Cheque 134257	45.00		
	Standing order	50.00		
	Cheque returned unpaid	200.00		10,890.00 CR

When the bank statement for the period is received the following steps should be followed for comparison with the cash book:

Step 1   Work through all of the receipts shown on the bank statement comparing each one to entries in the Bank receipts column in the cash book. When each receipt has been agreed to the Bank receipts column the entry on the bank statement and in the cash book should be ticked.

Step 2   Work through all of the payments shown on the bank statement comparing each one to entries in the Bank payments column in the cash book. When each receipt has been agreed to the Bank payments column the entry on the bank statement and in the cash book should be ticked.

Step 3   Any un-ticked items on the bank statement must be checked to ensure that the bank has not made a mistake.

Step 4   The un-ticked items on the bank statement can then be used to identify adjustments that are needed in the general ledger.

167

HOW IT WORKS

Anna Murphy has completed the process of checking her cash book to her bank statement. She is satisfied that the opening credit balance on the bank statement of £10,000 is correct but she has identified the following items that appear on the bank statement but do not appear in the cash book:

- A bank giro credit receipt from a customer with a customer code of SL876 for £2,400. She has discovered a remittance advice note from the customer which shows that £40 settlement discount was taken

- Bank charges of £15

- A BACS payment of net salaries of £1,200

- A cheque number 134257 paid for cash purchases (no VAT) of £45. In the bank payments column of the cash book a cheque with the same number appears with an amount of £54

- A standing order payment of £50. On checking with the bank Anna discovered that this was paid in error by the bank

- A cheque paid in for £200 from a customer with a customer code of SL452 has been dishonoured by the bank

It is possible that each of these points will require a journal entry to correct the general ledger accounts, and possibly also the memorandum sales and purchases ledgers.

Let us take each item in turn.

- **A bank giro credit receipt from a customer with a customer code of SL876 for £2,400. She has discovered a remittance advice note from the customer which shows that £40 settlement discount was taken**

Because a receipt by automated payment from a customer is not physically received as cash or a cheque by the business, it is very common for such items to appear on the bank statement before being entered in the cash book. Since this receipt and the discount taken have been validated by reference to the customer's remittance advice note, a journal to amend the cash book and other general ledger accounts can be prepared as follows:

Account name	Amount £	Debit (✓)	Credit (✓)
Bank	2,400	✓	
Sales ledger control	2,400		✓
Discounts allowed	40	✓	
Sales ledger control	40		✓

The sales ledger account SL876 also needs to be credited with £2,440 in total.

- **Bank charges of £15**

Bank charges are a cost to Anna's business so the journal entry needs to reflect this:

Account name	Amount £	Debit (✓)	Credit (✓)
Bank charges expense	15	✓	
Bank	15		✓

- **A BACS payment of net salaries of £1,200**

Payroll transactions are normally entered into the ledger accounts via the journal, so Anna needs to establish from the payroll exactly what entries should be made to record this payment in the general ledger. There is no doubt, however, that a payment by BACS (Bankers Automated Credit Service) should be credited to the bank payments column in the cash book.

- **A cheque number 134257 paid for £45. In the bank payments column of the cash book a cheque with the same number appears with an amount of £54**

Clearly the cheque should have been written in the cash book as £45 since this is the amount that the bank has paid out, so a journal entry needs to be made to correct the cash book and the purchases account. In the cash book £9 (£54 – £45) too much has been entered on the payments side, so the correcting journal is as follows:

Account name	Amount £	Debit (✓)	Credit (✓)
Bank	9	✓	
Purchases	9		✓

- **A standing order payment of £50. On checking with the bank Anna discovered that this was paid in error by the bank**

Although this payment has been made from Anna's bank account, reducing her balance by £50, it should not have been paid so it is up to the bank to process a correction. No correcting journal is needed for the ledger accounts.

- **A cheque paid in for £200 from a customer with a customer code of SL452 has been dishonoured by the bank**

When the cheque was entered in the cash book it would have been debited to bank and credited to sales ledger control. Now that the cheque has been dishonoured we must process a journal entry to remove the cash received and reinstate the debt:

Account name	Amount	Debit	Credit
	£	(✓)	(✓)
Sales ledger control	200	✓	
Bank	200		✓

The sales ledger account SL452 also needs to be debited with £200.

Task 1

The bank balance in D Ltd's cash book shows a debit balance of £12,450. The bank statement has the following items that do not appear in the cash book:

Standing order for rent of premises	400
BGC receipt from customer	230
Bank charges	25

Calculate the adjusted balance in D Ltd's cash book.

£ [   ]

Task 2

What is the journal entry for a cheque for £500 received from a customer and deposited with the bank but subsequently dishonoured?

Account name	Amount	Debit	Credit
	£	(✓)	(✓)

BANK RECONCILIATION STATEMENT

After correcting the cash book for all the legitimate items that appear on the bank statement we can calculate the correct balance for the bank account in the cash book. This does not mean however that the cash book balance will agree to that on the bank statement because we have not yet taken account of TIMING DIFFERENCES, the inevitable time lag between recording receipts and payments in the cash book and their appearance on the bank statement.

- Cash and cheques paid in by the business are recorded in the cash book but the clearing system means there is a delay before they appear on the bank statement. Such amounts are known as OUTSTANDING LODGEMENTS.

- When cheques are written to suppliers they are entered in the cash book immediately. The cheques are then sent to the supplier, the supplier must take them to the bank and then there will be a clearing period before they appear on the bank statement. Those cheque payments that are in the cash book but not on the bank statement yet are known as UNPRESENTED CHEQUES.

HOW IT WORKS

Anna Murphy has processed all the journals prepared above and her three column cash book as at 22 September is as follows (we are ignoring the analysis columns):

Details	Cash receipts	Bank receipts	Disc allowed	Details	Cheque number	Cash payments	Bank payments	Disc received
	£	£	£			£	£	£
Bal b/d	320.00	10,000.00		Supplier X	134255		700.00	
Customer A	400.00			Supplier Y	134256		480.00	
BGC		2,400.00	40.00	Bank charges			15.00	
Cash		720.00		BACS – salaries			1,200.00	
				Cash purchases	134257		45.00	
				Dishonoured cheque			200.00	
				Banking		720.00		
				Bal c/d			10,480.00	
	720.00	13,120.00	40.00			720.00	13,120.00	
Bal b/d		10,480.00						

We can now produce a BANK RECONCILIATION STATEMENT for Anna which will reconcile the corrected cash book balance for the bank account with the bank statement balance.

Firstly, we must remember to add back the standing order payment of £50 mistakenly made by the bank.

Next, by examining the Bank receipts column in the cash book we can see that there is an outstanding lodgement of cash and cheques for £720.00. This will increase the balance on the bank statement once they are recorded by the bank.

We can also see that there are two cheques which have not yet been paid out by the bank (cheque numbers 134255 and 134256). These are unpresented cheques which will make the bank statement figure smaller once they are paid. Therefore we deduct these in the bank reconciliation statement in order to come back to the cash book balance for the bank account of £10,480.00.

Bank reconciliation statement

	£	£
Balance per bank statement		10,890.00
Add back standing order payment made in error		50.00
Add outstanding lodgement		
Cash and cheques		720.00
Less unpresented cheques		
134255	700.00	
134256	480.00	
Total to subtract		(1,180.00)
Balance as per corrected cash book		10,480.00

Task 3

Which of the following will **not** appear in a bank reconciliation statement?

A   Unpresented cheques

B   Outstanding lodgements

C   Journal entries

D   Bank errors

CHAPTER OVERVIEW

- In order to check the accuracy of the bank columns in the cash book, it must be checked at regular intervals to the bank statements received

- The debit and credit entries and balances on the bank statement are the opposite to the entries in the ledger accounts as the bank is considering the accounting from its own perspective

- When checking the bank statement to the cash book, check each of the receipts and payments from the bank statement to the bank receipts and payments columns in the cash book and tick each agreed item in both the cash book and the bank statement

- Any un-ticked but valid items on the bank statement should be adjusted for in the general ledger (and the memorandum ledgers if necessary) by processing journal entries

- Once the relevant corrections have been made to the cash book it must be cast and balanced

- Any errors made by the bank which are highlighted must be adjusted by the bank and will also appear on the reconciliation

- The un-ticked items in the cash book are used to prepare the bank reconciliation statement

- The closing balance on the bank statement is reconciled to the corrected cash book balance in the bank reconciliation statement. The reconciling items will be bank errors, outstanding lodgements and unpresented cheques

Keywords

Outstanding lodgements – cheques that have been received and recorded in the cash receipts book but do not yet appear on the bank statement

Dishonoured cheque – cheque that is paid into a business's bank account and then is returned by the drawer's bank unpaid

Timing differences – the reason for the fact that the bank statement balance will rarely agree with the balance on the cash books, as receipts and payments recorded in the cash books will appear later in the bank statement due to the operation of the clearing system

Unpresented cheques – cheque payments that have been recorded in the cash payments book but do not yet appear on the bank statement

Bank reconciliation statement – a statement reconciling the bank statement balance to the corrected cash book balance

BPP
LEARNING MEDIA

TEST YOUR LEARNING

Test 1

While comparing the cash book to the bank statement the following differences have appeared. Prepare journal entries for the general ledger accounts as appropriate for each of these items.

(a) A receipt from a credit customer has been recorded in the cash receipts book as £310.50 but appears correctly on the bank statement as £301.50

Account name	Amount £	Debit (✓)	Credit (✓)

(b) Bank charges on the bank statement are £15.80

Account name	Amount £	Debit (✓)	Credit (✓)

(c) A direct debit payment is in the bank statement to English Gas Co for £300.00 but has not been recorded in the cash payments book

Account name	Amount £	Debit (✓)	Credit (✓)

Test 2

Given below is a business's cash receipts and payments book for the week ending 8 March, the bank statement for that week and the bank reconciliation statement for the week ended 1 March.

You are required to prepare the bank reconciliation statement for the week ending 8 March.

Bank reconciliation as at 8 March

	£
Balance per bank statement	
Add:	
Total to add:	
Less:	
Total to subtract:	
Balance as per cash book	

Cash Receipts Book

Date	Details	£
4 March	J Killick	365.37
	D Francis	105.48
5 March	I Oliver	216.57
6 March	L Canter	104.78
7 March	R Trent	268.59
8 March	P Otter	441.78
		1,502.57

Cash Payments Book

Date	Details	Cheque number	£
4 March	L L Partners	002536	186.90
	P J Parler	002537	210.55
5 March	J K Properties	002538	500.00
	Harmer & Co	002539	104.78
	Plenith Ltd	002540	60.80
7 March	Wessex & Co	002541	389.40
8 March	Filmer Partners	002542	104.67
			1,557.10

Bank reconciliation statement at 1 March

	£	£
Balance per bank statement		835.68
Less: unpresented cheques		
002530	110.46	
002534	230.56	
002535	88.90	
		(429.92)
		405.76
Add outstanding lodgement		102.45
Amended cash book balance		508.21

STATEMENT

first national
30 High Street
Benham
DR4 8TT

SOUTHFIELD ELECTRICAL LTD

CHEQUE ACCOUNT

Account number: 20-26-33 3126897

Sheet 023

Date		Paid out	Paid in	Balance
1 Mar	Balance b/f			835.68
4 Mar	Cheque no 002534	230.56		
	Credit		102.45	707.57
5 Mar	DD - National Telephones	145.00		
	Bank charges	7.80		554.77
6 Mar	Cheque No 002530	110.46		
	BACS - J T Turner		486.20	930.51
7 Mar	Credit		470.85	
	Cheque No 002537	210.55		
	Cheque No 002536	186.90		
	Cheque No 002538	500.00		503.91
8 Mar	Cheque No 002535	88.90		
	Credit		216.57	
	Cheque No 002539	104.78		526.80
8 Mar	Balance c/f			526.80

chapter 10:
CONTROL ACCOUNT RECONCILIATIONS

chapter coverage 📖

In this chapter we consider the reconciliations that are prepared for the sales ledger and purchases ledger control accounts with the sales and purchases ledgers, and the adjustments that may arise from the process.

The topics covered are:

✎ Sales ledger control account and the sales ledger

✎ Purchases ledger control account and the purchases ledger

✎ Control accounts

✎ Control account reconciliations

✎ Sales ledger control account reconciliation

✎ Purchases ledger control account reconciliation

SALES LEDGER CONTROL ACCOUNT AND THE SALES LEDGER

Before we look at the control account procedures and reconciliations we will firstly run through how the accounting system works for sales on credit.

Accounting system for sales on credit

The process of accounting for sales on credit is as follows:

- The sales invoices sent to customers are recorded in the sales day book.

- The total of the sales day book is regularly posted to the sales ledger control account.

- The individual invoices in the sales day book are posted to the individual customers' accounts in the memorandum sales ledger.

- Receipts from credit customers are recorded in the cash receipts book.

- The total of the cash receipts book is regularly posted to the sales ledger control account.

- The individual receipts are posted to the individual customer's account in the sales ledger.

HOW IT WORKS

Fred Simpson has recently set up in business and is not registered for VAT. He currently has just three credit customers Bill, John and Karen. His sales day book, sales ledger control account and memorandum sales ledger accounts for the month of June are given below.

Sales day book

Date	Customer	Invoice no.	Ref	£
3/06	Bill	0045	SL01	235.00
5/06	Karen	0046	SL03	141.00
8/06	John	0047	SL02	176.25
15/06	Karen	0048	SL03	258.50
20/06	John	0049	SL02	117.50
28/06	Bill	0050	SL01	211.50
				1,139.75

These figures must be posted to the sales ledger control account and the individual customers' accounts in the sales ledger:

General ledger

Sales ledger control account

	£		£
Balance b/d	587.50		
SDB	1,139.75		

Sales ledger

Bill   SL01

Date	Details	£	Date	Details	£
1/06	Balance b/d	235.00			
3/06	SDB 0045	235.00			
28/06	SDB 0050	211.50			

John   SL02

Date	Details	£	Date	Details	£
1/06	Balance b/d	117.50			
8/06	SDB 0047	176.25			
20/06	SDB 0049	117.50			

Karen   SL03

Date	Details	£	Date	Details	£
1/06	Balance b/d	235.00			
5/06	SDB 0046	141.00			
15/06	SDB 0048	258.50			

The totals of the opening balances on each individual account in the memorandum ledger add up to the opening balance on the sales ledger control account.

Opening balances

	£
Bill	235.00
John	117.50
Karen	235.00
Sales ledger control account	587.50

This should always be the case if the accounting has been correctly carried out – the totals of the balances at any point in time on the individual accounts in the sales ledger should be equal to the balance on the sales ledger control account.

Now we will deal with the receipts from these customers in the month of June:

Cash receipts book

Date	Details	Ref	Bank £	Discounts allowed £	Sales ledger £
6/06	John	SL02	117.50		117.50
10/06	Bill	SL01	225.60	9.40	225.60
13/06	Karen	SL03	200.00		200.00
20/06	Bill	SL01	225.60	9.40	225.60
28/06	Karen	SL03	100.00		100.00
30/06	John	SL02	176.25		176.25
			1,044.95	18.80	1,044.95

These figures must also be posted to the general ledger and the sales ledger, and the accounts must be balanced.

General ledger

Sales ledger control account

	£		£
Balance b/d	587.50	CRB	1,044.95
SDB	1,139.75	CRB – discounts	18.80
	1,727.25	Balance c/d	663.50
			1,727.25
Balance b/d	663.50		

Sales ledger

Bill   **SL01**

Date	Details	£	Date	Details	£
1/06	Balance b/d	235.00	10/06	CRB	225.60
3/06	SDB 0045	235.00	10/06	CRB – discount	9.40
28/06	SDB 0050	211.50	20/06	CRB	225.60
			20/06	CRB – discount	9.40
				Balance c/d	211.50
		681.50			681.50
Balance b/d		211.50			

John   SL02

Date	Details	£	Date	Details	£
1/06	Balance b/d	117.50	6/06	CRB	117.50
8/06	SDB 0047	176.25	30/06	CRB	176.25
20/06	SDB 0049	117.50	Balance c/d		117.50
		411.25			411.25
Balance b/d		117.50			

Karen   SL03

Date	Details	£	Date	Details	£
1/06	Balance b/d	235.00	13/06	CRB	200.00
5/06	SDB 0046	141.00	28/06	CRB	100.00
15/06	SDB 0048	258.50	Balance c/d		334.50
		634.50			634.50
Balance b/d		334.50			

Closing balances

The total of each of the individual customer balances equals the balance on the sales ledger control account at the end of June:

	£
Bill	211.50
John	117.50
Karen	334.50
Sales ledger control balance	663.50

If the double entry has all been correctly carried out then the total of the list of sales ledger balances will always equal the balance on the sales ledger control account.

PURCHASES LEDGER CONTROL ACCOUNT AND THE PURCHASES LEDGER

Accounting for credit purchases

The accounting process for credit purchases and suppliers is precisely the same as for credit customers except that the entries in the accounts are the other way around.

- The purchase invoices received are recorded in the purchases day book.

- The total of the purchases day book is regularly posted to the purchases ledger control account.

- Individual invoices in the purchases day book are posted to the individual suppliers' accounts in the memorandum purchases ledger.

- Payments to credit suppliers are recorded in the cash payments book.

- The total of the cash payments book is regularly posted to the purchases ledger control account.

- Individual payments are posted to the individual suppliers' accounts in the purchases ledger.

Closing balances

In just the same way as with the accounting system for credit customers, if the double entry has been correctly performed then the closing balances on the individual supplier accounts in the purchases ledger should total back to the balance on the purchases ledger control account.

CONTROL ACCOUNTS

We will now look in more detail at the figures that are likely to appear in the sales ledger and purchases ledger control accounts as so far we have only considered the basic entries for invoices and cash.

Sales ledger control account

A typical sales ledger control account might have the following entries:

Sales ledger control account

	£		£
Balance b/d	X	Sales returns	X
Credit sales	X	Receipts from credit customers	X
Dishonoured cheques	X	Discounts allowed	X
		Irrecoverable debts written off	X
		Contra entry	X
		Balance c/d	X
	X		X
Balance b/d	X		

Balance b/d – There is a debit opening balance on the account as the customers owe the business money. In some circumstances an individual customer may have a credit balance on their account in the sales ledger if they have overpaid, or are awaiting a credit note from the business for goods returned, but these would not show up separately on the control account.

Credit sales – This is the figure that is posted from the sales day book.

Dishonoured cheques – If a customer has paid for goods then there is a credit entry in the sales ledger control account but if the bank then returns the cheque as unpaid, ie the cheque has been 'dishonoured', the entry must be reversed by debiting the control account and crediting the bank account.

Sales returns – This is the posting from the sales returns day book.

Receipts from credit customers – This is the posting of the sales ledger column total from the cash receipts book.

Discounts allowed – This is the posting from the memorandum discounts allowed column in the cash receipts book.

Irrecoverable debts written off – This entry was covered in detail in Chapter 8.

Contra entry – A CONTRA ENTRY, sometimes known as a set off, comes about where a customer of the business is also its supplier ie we both sell to them and buy from them on credit. The contra entry is an amount owing by the customer which is set off against the amount we owe to them as a supplier. This will be dealt with in more detail later in the chapter.

Balance c/d and b/d – A debit balance is carried down on the credit side and brought down on the debit side.

Purchases ledger control account

A typical purchases ledger control account might look like this:

Purchases ledger control account

	£		£
		Balance b/d	X
Purchases returns	X	Credit purchases	X
Payments made to credit suppliers	X		
Discounts received	X		
Contra entry	X		
Balance c/d	X		
	X		X
		Balance b/d	X

Balance b/d – The balance brought down will be on the credit side of the account as we owe the suppliers money.

Purchases returns – This is the posting from the purchases returns day book.

Payments made to credit suppliers – This is the posting from the cash payments book.

Discounts received – This is the posting from the memorandum discounts received column total from the cash payments book.

Contra entry – This is the other side of the posting from the sales ledger control account – see below for more detail.

Credit purchases – This is the posting from the purchases day book.

Balance c/d and b/d – A credit balance is carried down on the debit side and brought down on the credit side.

Contra entries

It is entirely possible that a person or business can be both a receivables (debtor) and a payable (creditor) of your business at the same time. This would come about if your business makes credit sales to this person and buys goods on credit from the same person. If the business is owed money by this person and also owes money to them then it would make sense to net the two amounts off against each other and only pay or receive the difference. This is what a CONTRA ENTRY reflects.

HOW IT WORKS

Dawn Fisher sells goods on credit to Emma Jones and currently Emma owes Dawn £210. Dawn also sometimes buys goods on credit from Emma and currently Dawn owes Emma £100. The accounts for Emma in Dawn's sales ledger and purchases ledger appear as follows:

Sales ledger

Emma Jones			
	£		£
Balance b/d	210		

Purchases ledger

Emma Jones			
	£		£
		Balance b/d	100

Dawn and Emma have discussed this situation and have agreed that rather than Emma paying Dawn £210 and then Dawn paying Emma £100 it would be easier to net the two amounts off and for Emma simply to pay Dawn the remaining £110 that she owes.

This £100 will be debited to Emma's account in the purchases ledger and credited to her account in the sales ledger.

Sales ledger

Emma Jones			
	£		£
Balance b/d	210	Contra	100
		Balance c/d	110
	210		210
Balance b/d	110		

Purchases ledger

<table>
<tr><td colspan="4" align="center">**Emma Jones**</td></tr>
<tr><td></td><td align="right">£</td><td></td><td align="right">£</td></tr>
<tr><td>Contra</td><td align="right">100</td><td>Balance b/d</td><td align="right">100</td></tr>
</table>

This leaves Dawn with a balance of £110 on Emma's account in the sales ledger reflecting the agreed situation.

However if entries are made in the memorandum ledgers then they must also be reflected in the general ledger by a journal entry:

Account name	Amount	Debit	Credit
	£	(✓)	(✓)
Purchases ledger control	100	✓	
Sales ledger control	100		✓

General ledger

<table>
<tr><td colspan="4" align="center">**Sales ledger control account**</td></tr>
<tr><td></td><td align="right">£</td><td></td><td align="right">£</td></tr>
<tr><td></td><td></td><td>Contra</td><td align="right">100</td></tr>
</table>

<table>
<tr><td colspan="4" align="center">**Purchases ledger control account**</td></tr>
<tr><td></td><td align="right">£</td><td></td><td align="right">£</td></tr>
<tr><td>Contra</td><td align="right">100</td><td></td><td></td></tr>
</table>

Task 1

A business owes £500 to a supplier and that supplier also owes the business £800. They agree to net these amounts off.

Prepare the journal entry to reflect this agreement in the general ledger.

Account name	Debit £	Credit £

CONTROL ACCOUNT RECONCILIATIONS

We have seen that if all of the double entry in the general ledger and entries in the memorandum ledger are correctly carried out then the totals of the balances on the memorandum ledger should be equal to the balance on the control account.

Control account balances

The balances on the sales ledger and purchases ledger control accounts are the figures that will appear in the trial balance for receivables and payables and eventually in the financial statements. Therefore it is important to ensure that these figures are correct. This is done by carrying out a SALES LEDGER CONTROL ACCOUNT RECONCILIATION and a PURCHASES LEDGER CONTROL ACCOUNT RECONCILIATION.

The process involves comparing the balance on the control account to the total of the balances of the individual accounts in the memorandum ledger. If the two totals do not agree then there have been errors made in either the control account or the memorandum ledger or both. These errors must be investigated, discovered and corrected.

Some of the errors might have been made in the double entry in the general ledger so they affect the control account. Other errors might have been made when posting entries to the individual accounts in the memorandum ledger or in listing the balances in the memorandum ledger.

To summarise, the purpose of these reconciliations is to help:

- **Identify errors**
- **Identify omissions**

Errors affecting the control account

Typical types of errors that may have been made in the double entry in the general ledger, therefore affecting the control account balance may include the following:

- The books of prime entry may have been undercast or overcast so the incorrect total is posted to the control account (this would not affect the individual balances since these are posted with individual transactions from the books of prime entry).

- Postings from the books of prime entry may have been made to the wrong side of the control account.

- The discounts recorded in the cash book may be incorrectly treated in the control account.

- An irrecoverable debt may not have been entered into the general ledger although it was written off in the sales ledger.

- A contra entry may have been made in the memorandum ledgers but not entered into the general ledger accounts.

Errors affecting the list of balances

Some errors will not affect the double entry in the general ledger but will mean that the individual balances in the memorandum ledger are not correct or that these balances are listed and totalled incorrectly. Typical errors include the following:

- A transaction from the books of prime entry might be posted to the wrong account in the memorandum ledger.

- Entries from the books of prime entry may be posted to the wrong side of the memorandum ledger account.

- An entry from the books of prime entry may be posted as the wrong amount to the memorandum ledger account.

- A balance on an account in the memorandum ledger may be included in the list of balances as the wrong amount or as the wrong type of balance, eg a debit rather than a credit.

Task 2

If the sales day book total for a week is overcast by £1,000 this would affect the sales ledger control account/the individual accounts in the sales ledger.

SALES LEDGER CONTROL ACCOUNT RECONCILIATION

A sales ledger control account reconciliation is a comparison of the balance on the sales ledger control account to the total of the list of balances from the sales ledger to check for errors and omissions. This is carried out on a regular basis, usually monthly.

HOW IT WORKS

Dawn Fisher is carrying out her sales ledger control account reconciliation at the end of December 20X4. The balance on the sales ledger control account is £11,578. The total of the list of account balances from the sales ledger is £11,104.

Step 1   Check whether the control account total agrees to the total of the memorandum ledger balances.

	£
Control account total	11,578
List of balances	11,104
Difference	474

The reasons for this difference must be investigated.

Step 2   The control account and the individual accounts and balances must be checked and any errors or omissions noted.

In Dawn's case the following errors were noted:

(a)   A page of the cash receipts book had been undercast by £100

(b)   The total from the sales day book for a week had been posted as £2,340 instead of £2,430

(c)   An irrecoverable debt of £80 had been written off in the individual customer's account but not in the general ledger

(d)   An invoice to G Harper for £250 had been entered into the account of G Draper instead

(e)   A cash receipt from David Carr had been entered into his account as £175 instead of the correct figure from the cash receipts book of £157

(f)   A debit balance of £406 on one customer's account had been omitted from the list of balances

(g)   A credit balance of £20 on a customer's account had been included in the list of balances as a debit balance

Step 3   The accounts must be adjusted for any errors that affect them. We shall take each one in turn and identify the adjustment needed:

(a)   **A page of the cash receipts book had been undercast by £100**

The total from the cash receipts book would have been credited to the sales ledger control account so if it was undercast by £100 the account must be credited with a further £100.

Adjustment	Amount £	Debit (✓)	Credit (✓)
Sales ledger control	100		✓

(b) **The total from the sales day book for a week had been posted as £2,340 instead of £2,430**

The total from the sales day book is debited to the sales ledger control account and as the entry was for £90 too little an extra debit entry of £90 is required.

Adjustment	Amount £	Debit (✓)	Credit (✓)
Sales ledger control	90	✓	

(c) **An irrecoverable debt of £80 had been written off in the individual customer's account but not in the general ledger**

To write off an irrecoverable debt the sales ledger control account must be credited.

Adjustment	Amount £	Debit (✓)	Credit (✓)
Sales ledger control	80		✓

(d) **An invoice to G Harper for £250 had been entered into the account of G Draper instead**

This does not affect the sales ledger control account at all and also does not affect the total of the sales ledger balances – the correct amount was entered on the correct side, but in the wrong account.

(e) **A cash receipt from David Carr had been entered into his account as £175 instead of the correct figure from the cash receipts book of £157**

The receipt was recorded at a figure of £18 too much therefore the balance on this customer's account should be £18 higher.

Adjustment	Amount £	Debit (✓)	Credit (✓)
Sales ledger balances	18	✓	

(f) **A debit balance of £406 on one customer's account had been omitted from the list of balances**

The balance omitted must be added in to the total of the list of balances.

Adjustment	Amount £	Debit (✓)	Credit (✓)
Sales ledger balances	406	✓	

(g) **A credit balance of £20 on a customer's account had been included in the list of balances as a debit balance**

The error must be removed by removing the £20 debit balance, and then the correct credit balance of £20 must be entered, so in the end the correction is a £40 credit in the list of balances.

Adjustment	Amount £	Debit (✓)	Credit (✓)
Sales ledger balances	40		✓

Step 4 Process the adjustments to the sales ledger control account.

Sales ledger control account

	£		£
Balance b/d	11,578	(a) Cash receipts books	100
(b) Sales day book	90	(c) Irrecoverable debt	80
		Balance c/d	11,488
	11,668		11,668
Balance b/d	11,488		

Step 5 Adjust the total of the list of balances by adding or deducting the errors that affect this total.

	£
Original total	11,104
Add: (e) cash receipt adjustment (175 – 157)	18
(f) balance omitted	406
Less (g) credit balance included as debit balance	(40)
Amended total of the list of balances	11,488

The amended total of the list of balances now agrees to the amended sales ledger control account balance, and the general ledger and sales ledger are reconciled. The balance on the sales ledger control account can now be used as the receivables figure in the trial balance.

Task 3

The total of the discounts allowed column from the cash receipts book of £120 was not posted for a period. Set out the adjustment necessary in the sales ledger control account.

Adjustment	Amount £	Debit (✓)	Credit (✓)

PURCHASES LEDGER CONTROL ACCOUNT RECONCILIATION

A purchases ledger control account reconciliation works in exactly the same manner as a sales ledger control account reconciliation with the entries on the opposite sides, and no entry possible for irrecoverable debts.

HOW IT WORKS

Dawn Fisher is currently preparing her purchases ledger control account reconciliation at the end of October 20X4. The balance on the purchases ledger control account was £9,240 and the total of the list of balances from the purchases ledger was £9,040.

The following errors and omissions were noted:

(a) One page of the purchases day book has been undercast by £100.

(b) An invoice has been posted to an individual account in the purchases ledger as £863 instead of the correct figure from the purchases day book of £683.

(c) The total of discounts received of £160 was credited to the purchases ledger control account.

(d) One of the balances in the purchases ledger was included in the total at a figure of £235 instead of £325.

(e) A contra entry for £70 had been made in the purchases ledger but not in the general ledger.

Step 1   The accounts must be adjusted for any errors that affect them. We shall take each one in turn and identify the adjustment needed:

(a) **One page of the purchases day book has been undercast by £100**

The total from the purchases day book is credited to the purchases ledger control account and therefore if it was undercast by £100 then the account must be credited with £100.

Adjustment	Amount	Debit	Credit
	£	(✓)	(✓)
Purchases ledger control	100		✓

(b) **An invoice has been posted to an individual account in the purchases ledger as £863 instead of the correct figure from the purchases day book of £683**

An invoice would be posted to the credit side of the supplier's account – in this case it was posted at a figure £180 too high and therefore the balances would be reduced when the account was amended.

Adjustment	Amount £	Debit (✓)	Credit (✓)
Purchases ledger balances	180	✓	

(c) **The total of discounts received of £160 was credited to the purchases ledger control account**

The discounts received should have been debited to the purchases ledger control account – instead they were credited and therefore not only should there be one debit of £160 but two, one to cancel out the credit and one to put the debit entry in, therefore a debit of £320.

Adjustment	Amount £	Debit (✓)	Credit (✓)
Purchases ledger control	320	✓	

(d) **One of the balances in the purchases ledger was included in the total at a figure of £235 instead of £325**

The balance that was misstated was shown as £90 too small – therefore the balances need to be increased by £90.

Adjustment	Amount £	Debit (✓)	Credit (✓)
Purchases ledger balances	90		✓

(e) **A contra entry for £70 had been made in the purchases ledger but not in the general ledger**

The contra entry must be put into the purchases ledger control account as a debit of £70.

Adjustment	Amount £	Debit (✓)	Credit (✓)
Purchases ledger control	70	✓	

Step 2   Adjust the control account balance for the errors that affect it.

Purchases ledger control account

	£		£
		Balance b/d	9,240
(c) Discounts	320	(a) Purchases day book	100
(e) Contra	70		
Balance c/d	8,950		
	9,340		9,340
		Balance b/d	8,950

Step 3   Adjust the total of the list of balances for any errors that affect the individual balances or their total.

	£
Original total	9,040
Less (b) invoice misposting (863 – 683)	(180)
Add (e) balance misstated	90
	8,950

Now the amended balance on the purchases ledger control account of £8,950 agrees with the amended list of balances in the purchases ledger. This figure of £8,950 can now be used as the payables figure in the trial balance.

Task 4

An invoice for £350 was entered into the individual supplier's account in the purchases ledger on the wrong side of the account. How should this be adjusted for in the purchases ledger control account reconciliation?

Adjustment	Amount £	Debit (✓)	Credit (✓)

Task 5

Which of the following items will appear as an item posted to the purchases ledger control account?

A   Irrecoverable debts written off

B   Returns inwards of the period

C   Discounts allowed in total in the period

D   Discounts received in total in the period

Task 6

A business maintains a sales ledger control account. A debt of £1,500 is to be written off. Which of the following entries is correct (ignore VAT)?

A   Debit personal account of the customer, credit irrecoverable debts expense

B   Debit irrecoverable debts expense, credit sales ledger control

C   Debit sales ledger control, credit irrecoverable debt expense

D   Debit irrecoverable debts expense, credit personal account of the customer

CHAPTER OVERVIEW

- The sales ledger control account is debited with the sales invoices from the sales day book and credited with cash receipts and discounts from the cash receipts book

- The individual accounts for each customer in the sales ledger are also debited with each invoice total and credited with the cash and discounts

- If all of the entries are correctly carried out then the total of the closing balances on the individual accounts from the sales ledger should agree to the balance on the sales ledger control account

- The same system applies to accounting for credit suppliers although the entries are all on the opposite sides

- The sales ledger control account will potentially have entries for sales returns, dishonoured cheques, irrecoverable debts written off and contra entries as well as the basic entries for invoices, cash and discounts

- The purchases ledger control account will potentially have entries for purchases returns and a contra entry as well as the basic entries for invoices, cash and discounts

- A contra entry is caused by netting off a sales ledger and a purchases ledger balance with the same party – in the general ledger this is done by debiting the purchases ledger control account and crediting the sales ledger control account – in the memorandum ledgers the customer's account will be credited and the supplier's account debited

- If all of the entries in the general ledger and memorandum ledger have not been properly performed then the ledger balances total will not agree to the balance on the control account – in which case the errors that cause the difference must be discovered and adjusted

- When a control account reconciliation has been completed and adjustments have been made, the control account balance and the total of the list of balances should agree

Keywords

Contra entry – an amount owed by a customer which is set off against an amount owed to them as a supplier

Sales ledger control account reconciliation – an exercise which agrees the balance on the sales ledger control account to the total of the list of balances in the sales ledger

Purchases ledger control account reconciliation – an exercise which agrees the balance on the purchases ledger control account to the total of the list of balances in the purchases ledger

TEST YOUR LEARNING

Test 1

The balance on a business's sales ledger control account at the end of June was £41,774 and the total of the list of balances from the sales ledger came to £41,586.

The following errors were discovered:

(a) The sales day book was undercast by £100 on one page.

(b) A page from the sales returns day book with a total of £450 had not been posted to the control account although the individual returns had been recorded in the memorandum ledger.

(c) An invoice from the sales day book had been posted to the individual account of the customer as £769 instead of the correct figure of £679.

(d) A discount allowed to one customer of £16 had been posted to the wrong side of the customer's account in the sales ledger.

(e) An irrecoverable debt of £210 had been written off in the account in the sales ledger but not in the general ledger.

(f) A credit balance in the memorandum ledger of £125 had been included in the list of balances as a debit balance.

Use the following table to show the THREE adjustments you need to make to the sales ledger control account.

Adjustment	Amount £	Debit (✓)	Credit (✓)

Test 2

The balance on a business's purchases ledger control account at the end of June is £38,694 and the total of the list of balances in the memorandum purchases ledger came to £39,741.

The following errors were noted for the month:

(a) A page in the purchases returns day book was overcast by £300.

(b) A total from the cash payments book of £3,145 was posted in the general ledger as £3,415.

(c) Settlement discounts received from suppliers of £267 were omitted from both the general ledger and the purchases ledger.

(d) A credit note from a supplier for £210 was entered into the supplier's account in the purchases ledger as £120.

(e) A debit balance on an account in the purchases ledger of £187 was omitted from the list of balances.

(f) A credit balance in the purchases ledger should have been included in the list as £570 but instead was recorded as £770.

Use the following table to show the THREE adjustments you need to make to the purchases ledger control account.

Adjustment	Amount £	Debit (✓)	Credit (✓)

chapter 11:
THE TRIAL BALANCE, ERRORS AND THE SUSPENSE ACCOUNT

chapter coverage 📖

So far in this Text we have seen how to account for non-current assets and adjustments such as depreciation, accruals and prepayments, irrecoverable and doubtful debts and inventory. We have also looked at various reconciliations that are prepared at the end of an accounting period and how the errors that these identify can be adjusted. In Processing bookkeeping transactions we saw how to extract an initial trial balance and also how to redraft it if necessary. We now move on to look at how to complete a trial balance when taking into account the various adjustments that we have encountered.

In this chapter we first briefly revise the types of error that are found in ledger accounts, and whether they cause a suspense account on the trial balance or not. We then work through an example showing how to go from the year end balances for a sole trader to the completed trial balance via an initial trial balance and various accounting adjustments. In doing so we cover accounting for errors using the suspense account.

The topics covered are:

✍ Types of error

✍ Completing the trial balance

TYPES OF ERROR

In any accounting system there are several types of error that can be made when making entries to the ledger accounts. Some of these will be identified when reconciliations are prepared, as we saw in Chapters 9 and 10, and some will come to light when a trial balance is extracted. There are also, however, a number of types of error that do not affect the balancing of the trial balance – despite the error, the trial balance will still balance.

Errors leading to an imbalance on the trial balance

The following types of error will mean that the debit balances on the trial balance do not equal the credit balances, so a suspense account must be opened and cleared.

Type of error	Description	Correction	Example
One-sided entry	Only one side of the double entry has been made in the ledger accounts, eg the debit and not the credit	Make the missing entry and post the other side to the suspense account	*Error* £10 cash purchase only credited to cash *Correction* Debit Purchases £10 Credit Suspense £10
Entry duplicated on one side, nothing on the other	Instead of posting a transaction as a debit in one account and a credit in another, both accounts are posted with debit entries, or both with credit entries. One account is correct but the other is out of balance by twice the amount of the posting	Post the account that was posted on the wrong side with twice the amount, and post the other side to suspense	*Error* £10 cash purchase credited to both cash and purchases *Correction* Debit Purchases £20 Credit Suspense £20

Type of error	Description	Correction	Example
Unequal entries, normally caused by a transposition error	The correct amount is entered on one side, but there is an error in writing in the other side of the entry. Often this is caused by a transposition error in the incorrect entry, where the digits in a number are transposed (swapped round). If this is the only error in the accounts then the difference between the debits and the credits will be divisible by 9	In the account with the wrong posting, post an amount to bring the entry to the right amount, and post the other side to suspense	*Error* £10 cash purchase debited to purchases as £100 (correct credit to cash) *Correction* Debit Suspense £90 Credit Purchases £90
Account balance incorrectly transferred to the trial balance	This may be because of a calculation error when calculating the balance on a ledger account, or it may be that a balance which has been calculated correctly in the ledger is entered incorrectly to the trial balance	In the account with the wrong balance, post an amount to bring the balance to the right amount, and post the other side to suspense	*Error* £1,000 debit balance on purchases account written into trial balance as a £100 debit balance *Correction* Debit Purchases £900 Credit Suspense £900

Type of error	Description	Correction	Example
Balance omission	A balance on a general ledger account is omitted from the trial balance completely	Enter the missing balance on the correct side and enter the suspense account with the same amount on the other side	*Error* £1,000 debit balance on purchases account omitted *Correction* Debit Purchases on trial balance £1,000 Credit Suspense on trial balance £1,000

Errors not revealed by an imbalance on the trial balance

Unfortunately, there are also some types of error that do not cause a difference on the trial balance and therefore cannot be revealed through the trial balance process – though they must still be found of course!

Type of error	Description	Correction	Example
Error of principle	The double entry is arithmetically correct but the wrong type of account has been used eg a non-current asset account is debited with expenses	Remove the incorrect entry and post it to the correct account	*Error* Motor expenses of £100 have been debited to the motor vehicles cost account *Correction* Debit Motor expenses £100 Credit Motor vehicles cost £100

Type of error	Description	Correction	Example
Error of original entry	Both the debit and the credit entries have been made using the wrong amount because: – The transaction was recorded in the book of prime entry at the incorrect amount, or – The wrong figure was picked up from the primary record (eg a transposition error was made), this incorrect figure was used to write up the book of prime entry and so to make both the debit and the credit entry	In both accounts, post an amount to bring the entry to the right amount	*Error* Motor expenses of £100 have been recorded as £10 in the purchases day book *Correction* Debit Motor expenses £90 Credit Purchases ledger control £90
Error of omission	A transaction is completely omitted from the ledger accounts	Make the appropriate posting	*Error* Cash purchases of £10 have not been recorded *Correction* Debit Purchases £10 Credit Cash £10

Type of error	Description	Correction	Example
Reversal of entries	The correct figure has been used and a debit and a credit entry made but the debit and the credit are on the wrong side of the respective accounts	Remove the incorrect entries and make the correct ones by posting the accounts correctly but with double the amount	*Error* Cash purchases of £10 have been debited to cash and credited to purchases *Correction* Debit Purchases £20 Credit Cash £20
Error of commission	The double entry is arithmetically correct but a wrong account of the same type has been used eg a phone expense is debited to the electricity account rather than the phone account	Remove the incorrect entry and post it to the correct account	*Error* Motor expenses of £100 have been debited to the office expenses account *Correction* Debit Motor expenses £100 Credit Office expenses £100

COMPLETING THE TRIAL BALANCE

We will now work through a comprehensive example which will take you from ledger account balances through to a completed trial balance via adjustments and a suspense account.

HOW IT WORKS

Given below are the brought down balances on the ledger accounts at the end of the day on 31 March 20X4, the year end, for John Thompson, who is not registered for VAT.

Building at cost

		£			£
31 Mar	Balance b/d	100,000			

Furniture and fittings at cost

		£			£
31 Mar	Balance b/d	4,800			

Motor vehicles at cost

		£			£
31 Mar	Balance b/d	32,700			

Computer at cost

		£			£
31 Mar	Balance b/d	2,850			

Accumulated depreciation – building

	£			£
		31 Mar	Balance b/d	4,000

Accumulated depreciation – furniture and fittings

	£			£
		31 Mar	Balance b/d	1,920

Accumulated depreciation – motor vehicles

	£			£
		31 Mar	Balance b/d	7,850

Accumulated depreciation – computer

	£			£
		31 Mar	Balance b/d	950

Inventory

		£			£
31 Mar	Balance b/d	4,400			

Bank/cash

		£			£
31 Mar	Balance b/d	3,960			

Petty cash

		£			£
31 Mar	Balance b/d	100			

Sales ledger control

		£			£
31 Mar	Balance b/d	15,240			

Purchases ledger control

		£			£
			31 Mar	Balance b/d	5,010

Capital

		£			£
			31 Mar	Balance b/d	130,000

Sales revenue

		£			£
			31 Mar	Balance b/d	155,020

Sales returns

		£			£
31 Mar	Balance b/d	2,100			

Purchases

		£			£
31 Mar	Balance b/d	80,200			

Purchases returns

		£			£
			31 Mar	Balance b/d	1,400

Bank charges

		£			£
31 Mar	Balance b/d	200			

Discounts allowed

		£			£
31 Mar	Balance b/d	890			

Discounts received

		£			£
			31 Mar	Balance b/d	1,260

Wages

		£			£
31 Mar	Balance b/d	32,780			

Rates

		£			£
31 Mar	Balance b/d	5,500			

Telephone

		£			£
31 Mar	Balance b/d	1,140			

Electricity

		£			£
31 Mar	Balance b/d	1,480			

Insurance

		£			£
31 Mar	Balance b/d	1,500			

Motor expenses

		£			£
31 Mar	Balance b/d	1,580			

Office expenses

		£			£
31 Mar	Balance b/d	960			

Allowance for doubtful debts

		£			£
			31 Mar	Balance b/d	220

Loan

		£			£
			31 Mar	Balance b/d	820

Drawings

		£			£
31 Mar	Balance b/d	15,800			

The first stage is to transfer all of the closing balances on the ledger accounts to the trial balance, add it up and check that it balances. If it does not balance, first check your additions and if this doesn't clear it, then open up a suspense account to make the debits and credits equal.

Draft trial balance as at 31 March 20X4

	Debit £	Credit £
Buildings at cost	100,000	
Furniture and fittings at cost	4,800	
Motor vehicles at cost	32,700	
Computer at cost	2,850	
Accumulated depreciation – buildings		4,000
Accumulated depreciation – furniture and fittings		1,920
Accumulated depreciation – motor vehicles		7,850
Accumulated depreciation – computer		950
Inventory	4,400	
Bank/cash	3,960	
Petty cash	100	
Sales ledger control	15,240	
Purchases ledger control		5,010
Capital		130,000
Sales revenue		155,020
Sales returns	2,100	
Purchases	80,200	
Purchases returns		1,400
Bank charges	200	
Discounts allowed	890	
Discounts received		1,260
Wages	32,780	
Rates	5,500	
Telephone	1,140	
Electricity	1,480	
Insurance	1,500	
Motor expenses	1,580	
Office expenses	960	
Allowance for doubtful debts		220
Loan		820
Drawings	15,800	
Suspense	270	
	308,450	308,450

Suspense account

In this case the credit total was £270 larger than the debit total and so a suspense account was opened for the difference. The suspense account must of course be cleared and the errors that were discovered are given below:

(a) The purchases returns account was overcast by £100.

(b) £200 of office expenses has been charged to the motor expenses account.

(c) Discounts allowed of £170 have been correctly accounted for in the sales ledger control account but omitted from the discounts allowed account.

We must now prepare journal entries to correct these errors and to clear the suspense account.

Journal entries

(a) As purchase returns are a credit balance if the account has been overstated then the purchases returns account must be debited and the suspense account credited.

Account name	Amount £	Debit (✓)	Credit (✓)
Purchases returns	100	✓	
Suspense	100		✓

(b) The motor expenses account has been wrongly debited with office expenses so the motor expenses account must be credited and office expenses debited.

Account name	Amount £	Debit (✓)	Credit (✓)
Office expenses	200	✓	
Motor expenses	200		✓

(c) The correct double entry for discounts allowed is a debit to the discounts allowed account and a credit to sales ledger control. The credit has been done but the debit is missing. Therefore we must debit discounts allowed and credit the suspense account.

Account name	Amount £	Debit (✓)	Credit (✓)
Discounts allowed	170	✓	
Suspense	170		✓

Year end adjustments

You are also given information about the following year end adjustments that must be made:

(a) Depreciation is to be charged for the year using the following depreciation policy:

- Building – 2% straight line
- Furniture and fittings – 20% straight line
- Motor vehicles – 30% reducing balance
- Computer – 33⅓ % straight line

(b) Rates of £500 are to be accrued.

(c) The insurance account includes an amount of £300 that relates to the year ended 31 March 20X5.

(d) An irrecoverable debt of £240 is to be written off.

(e) An allowance for 2% of the remaining debts is required.

We must now prepare the journal entries that will complete these adjustments and close off the accounts for the period.

Journal entries

(a) The accumulated depreciation accounts in the trial balance are as at the beginning of the year since the annual depreciation charge has yet to be accounted for. In each case the double entry is to debit a depreciation charge account and to credit the relevant accumulated depreciation account.

	Debit £	Credit £
Depreciation charge – building (100,000 × 2%)	2,000	
Accumulated depreciation – building		2,000
Depreciation charge – furniture and fittings (4,800 × 20%)	960	
Accumulated depreciation – furniture and fittings		960
Depreciation charge – motor vehicles ((32,700 – 7,850) × 30%)	7,455	
Accumulated depreciation – motor vehicles		7,455
Depreciation charge – computer (2,850 × 33⅓)	950	
Accumulated depreciation – computer		950

(b)   Rates of £500 are to be accrued.

	Debit £	Credit £
Rates	500	
Accruals		500

(c)   Insurance has been prepaid by £300.

	Debit £	Credit £
Prepayments	300	
Insurance		300

(d)   An irrecoverable debt of £240 is to be written off.

	Debit £	Credit £
Irrecoverable debts expense	240	
Sales ledger control		240

(e)   An allowance for doubtful debts of 2% of the remaining debts is required.

	£
Allowance required = (15,240 – 240) × 2%	300
Current level of allowance	220
Increase in allowance	80

	Debit £	Credit £
Allowance for doubtful debts adjustment	80	
Allowance for doubtful debts		80

Closing inventory

The closing inventory has been counted and valued at £5,200.

The inventory figure in the draft trial balance is the opening inventory which will eventually be debited to the statement of profit or loss as part of cost of sales. The closing inventory must now be entered into the accounts with a journal entry.

	Debit £	Credit £
Inventory – statement of financial position	5,200	
Inventory – statement of profit or loss		5,200

Updating ledger accounts

All the journal entries have now been made for the correction of errors, adjustments and closing inventory. These journals must now be entered into the ledger accounts and the ledger accounts balanced to give their amended closing balances. This means that a number of new ledger accounts have to be opened.

Errors

(a)

Purchases returns

		£			£
31 March	Journal	100	31 March	Balance b/d	1,400
31 March	Balance c/d	1,300			
		1,400			1,400
			31 March	Balance b/d	1,300

Suspense account

		£			£
31 March	Balance b/d	270	31 March	Journal	100

(b)

Office expenses

		£			£
31 March	Balance b/d	960			
31 March	Journal	200	31 March	Balance c/d	1,160
		1,160			1,160
31 March	Balance b/d	1,160			

Motor expenses

		£			£
31 March	Balance b/d	1,580	31 March	Journal	200
			31 March	Balance c/d	1,380
		1,580			1,580
31 March	Balance b/d	1,380			

(c)

Discounts allowed

		£			£
31 March	Balance b/d	890			
31 March	Journal	170	31 March	Balance c/d	1,060
		1,060			1,060
31 March	Balance b/d	1,060			

Suspense account

		£			£
31 March	Balance b/d	270	31 March	Journal	100
			31 March	Journal	170
		270			270

Year end adjustments

(a) Depreciation charges for the year

Depreciation charge – building

		£		£
31 March	Journal	2,000		

Accumulated depreciation – building

		£			£
			31 March	Balance b/d	4,000
31 March	Balance c/d	6,000	31 March	Journal	2,000
		6,000			6,000
			31 March	Balance b/d	6,000

Depreciation charge – furniture and fittings

		£		£
31 March	Journal	960		

Accumulated depreciation – furniture and fittings

		£			£
			31 March	Balance b/d	1,920
31 March	Balance c/d	2,880	31 March	Journal	960
		2,880			2,880
			31 March	Balance b/d	2,880

Depreciation charge – motor vehicles

		£		£
31 March	Journal	7,455		

Accumulated depreciation – motor vehicles

		£			£
			31 March	Balance b/d	7,850
31 March	Balance c/d	15,305	31 March	Journal	7,455
		15,305			15,305
			31 March	Balance b/d	15,305

Depreciation charge – computer

		£		£
31 March	Journal	950		

Accumulated depreciation – computer

		£			£
			31 March	Balance b/d	950
31 March	Balance c/d	1,900	31 March	Journal	950
		1,900			1,900
			31 March	Balance b/d	1,900

(b)   Rates accrual

Rates

		£			£
31 March	Balance b/d	5,500			
31 March	Journal	500	31 March	Balance c/d	6,000
		6,000			6,000
31 March	Balance b/d	6,000			

Accruals

		£			£
			31 March	Journal	500

(c)   Insurance prepaid

Insurance

		£			£
31 March	Balance b/d	1,500	31 March	Journal	300
			31 March	Balance c/d	1,200
		1,500			1,500
31 March	Balance b/d	1,200			

Prepayments

		£			£
31 March	Journal	300			

(d)   Irrecoverable debt write off

Irrecoverable debts expense

		£			£
31 March	Journal	240			

Sales ledger control

		£			£
31 March	Balance b/d	15,240	31 March	Journal	240
			31 March	Balance c/d	15,000
		15,240			15,240
31 March	Balance b/d	15,000			

(e)   Allowance for doubtful debts

Allowance for doubtful debts adjustment

		£			£
31 March	Journal	80			

Allowance for doubtful debts

		£			£
			31 March	Balance b/d	220
31 March	Balance c/d	300	31 March	Journal	80
		300			300
			31 March	Balance b/d	300

Closing inventory

Inventory – statement of financial position

	£		£
31 March Journal	5,200		

Inventory – statement of profit or loss

	£			£
		31 March	Journal	5,200

Once all the ledger accounts have been updated for the journal entries a new final trial balance is drawn up which reflects all of the error corrections and adjustments.

Note that we now have three inventory account balances. Do not worry about this at the moment as it will be explained in Chapter 12.

Final trial balance as at 31 March 20X4

	Debit £	Credit £
Buildings at cost	100,000	
Furniture and fittings at cost	4,800	
Motor vehicles at cost	32,700	
Computer at cost	2,850	
Accumulated depreciation – buildings		6,000
Accumulated depreciation – furniture and fittings		2,880
Accumulated depreciation – motor vehicles		15,305
Accumulated depreciation – computer		1,900
Inventory at 1 April 20X3	4,400	
Bank/cash	3,960	
Petty cash	100	
Sales ledger control	15,000	
Purchases ledger control		5,010
Capital		130,000
Sales revenue		155,020
Sales returns	2,100	
Purchases	80,200	
Purchases returns		1,300
Bank charges	200	
Discounts allowed	1,060	
Discounts received		1,260
Wages	32,780	
Rates	6,000	
Telephone	1,140	
Electricity	1,480	
Insurance	1,200	
Motor expenses	1,380	
Office expenses	1,160	
Allowance for doubtful debts		300
Loan		820
Drawings	15,800	
Suspense	–	
Depreciation charge – building	2,000	
Depreciation charge – furniture and fittings	960	
Depreciation charge – motor vehicles	7,455	
Depreciation charge – computer	950	
Accruals		500
Prepayments	300	
Irrecoverable debts expense	240	
Allowance for doubtful debts adjustment	80	
Inventory – statement of financial position	5,200	
Inventory – statement of profit or loss		5,200
	325,495	325,495

Final ledger account adjustments

Once the balances on the trial balance have been taken to the statement of profit or loss and statement of financial position there is one final set of adjustments that must be done to some of the ledger accounts.

The income and expense ledger accounts must be closed off as the balances are no longer required in the ledger. This is done by taking the balances on each individual income and expense ledger account to a new ledger account known as the STATEMENT OF PROFIT OR LOSS LEDGER ACCOUNT.

HOW IT WORKS

The final balances on the sales revenue account, purchases account and wages account are shown below.

Sales revenue

	£		£
		Balance b/d	155,020

Purchases

	£		£
Balance b/d	80,200		

Wages

	£		£
Balance b/d	32,780		

These accounts must be closed off ready to start with a clean sheet at the beginning of the next accounting period. This is done by transferring the balances remaining to the statement of profit or loss ledger account.

Sales revenue

	£		£
Statement of profit or loss	155,020	Balance b/d	155,020

Purchases

	£		£
Balance b/d	80,200	Statement of profit or loss	80,200

Wages

	£		£
Balance b/d	32,780	Statement of profit or loss	32,780

Statement of profit or loss

	£		£
Purchases	80,200	Sales	155,020
Wages	32,780		

This will be done for all statement of profit or loss balances and there will need to be journal entries for each of these final adjustments. Therefore the final set of journal entries in full will be as follows:

Journal entries

	Debit £	Credit £
Opening inventory		
Statement of profit or loss	4,400	
Inventory		4,400
Sales revenue		
Sales revenue	155,020	
Statement of profit or loss		155,020
Sales returns		
Statement of profit or loss	2,100	
Sales returns		2,100
Purchases		
Statement of profit or loss	80,200	
Purchases		80,200
Purchases returns		
Purchases returns	1,300	
Statement of profit or loss		1,300
Bank charges		
Statement of profit or loss	200	
Bank charges		200
Discounts allowed		
Statement of profit or loss	1,060	
Discounts allowed		1,060
Discounts received		
Discounts received	1,260	
Statement of profit or loss		1,260
Wages		
Statement of profit or loss	32,780	
Wages		32,780
Rates		
Statement of profit or loss	6,000	
Rates		6,000

	Debit £	Credit £
Telephone		
Statement of profit or loss	1,140	
Telephone		1,140
Electricity		
Statement of profit or loss	1,480	
Electricity		1,480
Insurance		
Statement of profit or loss	1,200	
Insurance		1,200
Motor expenses		
Statement of profit or loss	1,380	
Motor expenses		1,380
Office expenses		
Statement of profit or loss	1,160	
Office expenses		1,160
Depreciation charge – buildings		
Statement of profit or loss	2,000	
Depr'n charge – buildings		2,000
Depreciation charge – furniture and fittings		
Statement of profit or loss	960	
Depr'n charge – furniture and fittings		960
Depreciation charge – motor vehicles		
Statement of profit or loss	7,455	
Depr'n charge – motor vehicles		7,455
Depreciation charge – computer		
Statement of profit or loss	950	
Depr'n charge – computer		950
Irrecoverable debt expense		
Statement of profit or loss	240	
Irrecoverable debts expense		240
Allowance for doubtful debts adjustment		
Statement of profit or loss	80	
Allowance for doubtful debts adjustment		80
Inventory – statement of profit or loss		
Inventory – statement of profit or loss	5,200	
Statement of profit or loss		5,200

Statement of financial position ledger account balances

There is no need to do any similar adjustments to statement of financial position ledger accounts ie assets and liabilities. This is because they remain as opening balances for the following accounting period in the ledger account. For example, the closing balance on the Buildings at cost account is £100,000 and this is the balance brought down or opening balance for the buildings at the start of the next accounting period.

Task 1

What are the year-end journal entries required to clear the following accounts:

(a)   Purchases returns account

Account name	Debit (✓)	Credit (✓)

(b)   Insurance account

Account name	Debit (✓)	Credit (✓)

(c)   Sales ledger control account

Account name	Debit (✓)	Credit (✓)

Task 2

Which of the following is an example of an error of commission where no control account is kept?

A   A receipt of £25 from J Gee entered in G Jay's account as a credit and debited to cash

B   A purchase of cleaning materials recorded as DR cash £50, CR cleaning materials £50

C   An invoice for £1,300 is lost and not recorded at all

D   An invoice for £2,500 sales is posted as £2,050

Task 3

Which of the following errors would be a possible reason for the trial balance not balancing?

A   Sales of £500 entered correctly but entered as £1,500 in the sales ledger control account

B   A purchase of £550 on credit not being recorded

C   Cash wages being recorded as DR cash £250, CR wages £250

D   A non-current asset purchase of £750 being recorded ad DR machinery repairs £750, CR cash £750

CHAPTER OVERVIEW

- Start by preparing an initial trial balance from the closing ledger account balances – you may need to set up a suspense account balance if the trial balance does not initially balance

- The suspense account must be cleared by journal entries to correct any errors identified

- Make journal entries for the period end adjustments for depreciation, accruals, prepayments, irrecoverable and doubtful debts and closing inventory

- Update the ledger account balances for the adjustments and corrections and prepare a final trial balance

- As a final year end adjustment all income and expense balances must be cleared out to the statement of profit or loss ledger account

TEST YOUR LEARNING

Test 1

The phone expense and insurance expense accounts of a sole trader have balances of £3,400 and £1,600 respectively at 30 September. However £300 of phone expense is to be accrued and £200 of insurance has been prepaid. What are the final expense figures that will appear in the statement of profit or loss for the year to 30 September?

Phone expense   £ [   ]

Insurance expense   £ [   ]

chapter 12:
THE EXTENDED TRIAL BALANCE

chapter coverage 📖

Accounts Preparation requires you to use the extended trial balance in order to help prepare the financial statements. This technique builds on the trial balance and the preparation of adjustments in order to let us see whether balances are going into the statement of profit or loss or the statement of financial position. It also helps in the calculation of the period's profit or loss.

The topics covered are:

✍ Extended trial balance

✍ How to prepare the extended trial balance

✍ Disposals and the ETB

EXTENDED TRIAL BALANCE

In this chapter we introduce the EXTENDED TRIAL BALANCE. The extended trial balance (ETB) is a technique that allows the initial trial balance to be adjusted for the necessary year end adjustments, to be corrected for any errors that are found and eventually to form the basis for the preparation of the financial statements.

An extended trial balance will normally have a column for the account name followed by eight further working columns:

Extended trial balance

Account name	Ledger balances		Adjustments		Statement of profit or loss		Statement of financial position	
	DR	CR	DR	CR	DR	CR	DR	CR

HOW TO PREPARE THE EXTENDED TRIAL BALANCE

We will start with a summary of the procedure for preparing an extended trial balance (ETB) and then work through it on a step by step basis.

Step 1   Enter each ledger account balance as either a debit or a credit in the ledger balance column. This is the initial trial balance and it should balance – however if there is a difference between the debits and the credits a suspense account balance should be added to make the trial balance add up. Leave a number of empty lines at the bottom of this trial balance before totalling it as these will be necessary for adjustments and corrections.

Step 2   If there is a suspense account, deal with the errors that have caused this by entering the debits and credits to correct the errors in the adjustments column.

Step 3   Enter any year end adjustments as directed in the adjustments column such as: the depreciation charge for the year, closing inventory, accruals and prepayments, irrecoverable debts written off and adjustments for allowance for doubtful debts. When doing this you may need to open up some new account lines in the ETB in the blank lines that you have left at the bottom of the ETB.

Step 4   Total and extend each line of the ETB into the statement of profit or loss or statement of financial position columns as appropriate.

Step 5   Total the statement of profit or loss columns. The difference is the profit or loss for the year. Enter this amount twice:

- In the appropriate column to make the statement of profit or loss columns balance; and

- In the opposite statement of financial position column; then

- Total the statement of financial position columns – they should be equal.

HOW IT WORKS

We will use the example of John Thompson used in Chapter 11.

Given below is the list of ledger balances for John Thompson, a wholesaler of small electrical items, at his year end of 31 March 20X4.

	£
Buildings at cost	100,000
Furniture and fittings at cost	4,800
Motor vehicles at cost	32,700
Computer at cost	2,850
Accumulated depreciation at 1 April 20X3	
– buildings	4,000
– furniture and fittings	1,920
– motor vehicles	7,850
– computer	950
Inventory at 1 April 20X3	4,400
Bank/cash (debit balance)	3,960
Petty cash	100
Sales ledger control	15,240
Purchases ledger control	5,010
Capital	130,000
Sales revenue	155,020
Sales returns	2,100
Purchases	80,200
Purchases returns	1,400
Bank charges	200
Discounts allowed	890
Discounts received	1,260
Wages	32,780
Rates	5,500
Telephone	1,140
Electricity	1,480
Insurance	1,500
Motor expenses	1,580
Office expenses	960
Allowance for doubtful debts at 1 April 20X3	220
Loan	820
Drawings	15,800

Step 1   Enter these balances onto the ETB in the debit and credit columns of the ledger balance columns. Total the trial balance and check your totals carefully. Enter a suspense account balance if necessary.

Extended trial balance

Account name	Ledger balances		Adjustments		SPL		SFP	
	DR £	CR £	DR £	CR £	DR £	CR £	DR £	CR £
Buildings at cost	100,000							
Furniture and fittings at cost	4,800							
Motor vehicles at cost	32,700							
Computer at cost	2,850							
Accumulated depreciation at 1 April 20X3:								
– buildings		4,000						
– furniture and fittings		1,920						
– motor vehicles		7,850						
– computer		950						
Inventory at 1 April 20X3	4,400							
Bank/cash	3,960							
Petty cash	100							
Sales ledger control	15,240							
Purchases ledger control		5,010						
Capital		130,000						
Sales revenue		155,020						
Sales returns	2,100							
Purchases	80,200							
Purchases returns		1,400						
Bank charges	200							
Discounts allowed	890							
Discounts received		1,260						
Wages	32,780							
Rates	5,500							
Telephone	1,140							
Electricity	1,480							
Insurance	1,500							
Motor expenses	1,580							
Office expenses	960							
Allowance for doubtful debts at 1 April 20X3		220						
Loan		820						
Drawings	15,800							
Suspense account	270							
	308,450	308,450						

In this case the trial balance does not balance. The total of the debit column is £308,180 and the total of the credit column is £308,450, so a suspense account balance of £270 is entered into the debit column in order to make the trial balance add up.

Take note of some of the entries in the trial balance. The accumulated depreciation and allowance for doubtful debts are as at 1 April 20X3. This means that the depreciation charge for the year has not yet been accounted for, nor has there been any adjustment to the allowance for receivables for the year.

The inventory figure in the trial balance is also as at 1 April 20X3, as it is the opening inventory. The inventory figure in the trial balance is always the opening inventory figure as the closing inventory is not entered into the accounts until the year end when it is counted and valued (see Chapter 7).

Step 2   Deal with the errors that have caused the balance on the suspense account. The errors that have been found are given below:

- The purchases returns account was overcast by £100

| Debit | Purchases returns | £100 |
| Credit | Suspense | £100 |

- £200 of office expenses has been charged to the motor expenses account

| Debit | Office expenses | £200 |
| Credit | Motor expenses | £200 |

- Discounts allowed of £170 had been correctly accounted for in the sales ledger control account but omitted from the discounts allowed account

| Debit | Discounts allowed | £170 |
| Credit | Suspense | £170 |

These three double entries will now be entered into the ETB.

Account name	Ledger balances DR £	Ledger balances CR £	Adjustments DR £	Adjustments CR £	SPL DR £	SPL CR £	SFP DR £	SFP CR £
Buildings at cost	100,000							
Furniture and fittings at cost	4,800							
Motor vehicles at cost	32,700							
Computer at cost	2,850							
Accumulated depreciation at 1 April 20X3:								
– buildings		4,000						
– furniture and fittings		1,920						
– motor vehicles		7,850						
– computer		950						
Inventory at 1 April 20X3	4,400							
Bank/cash	3,960							
Petty cash	100							
Sales ledger control	15,240							
Purchases ledger control		5,010						
Capital		130,000						
Sales revenue		155,020						
Sales returns	2,100							
Purchases	80,200							
Purchases returns		1,400	100					
Bank charges	200							
Discounts allowed	890		170					
Discounts received		1,260						
Wages	32,780							
Rates	5,500							
Telephone	1,140							
Electricity	1,480							
Insurance	1,500							
Motor expenses	1,580			200				
Office expenses	960		200					
Allowance for doubtful debts at 1 April 20X3		220						
Loan		820						
Drawings	15,800							
Suspense account	270			100 + 170				
	308,450	308,450						

Step 3 Enter the year end adjustments in the adjustments columns:

(a) Depreciation

    (i) Buildings – 2% straight line

        £100,000 × 2% = £2,000

Debit	Buildings depreciation charge	£2,000
Credit	Buildings accumulated depreciation	£2,000

    (ii) Furniture and fittings – 20% straight line

        £4,800 × 20% = £960

Debit	Furniture depreciation charge	£960
Credit	Furniture accumulated depreciation	£960

    (iii) Motor vehicles – 30% reducing balance

        (£32,700 – 7,850) × 30% = £7,455

Debit	Vehicles depreciation charge	£7,455
Credit	Vehicles accumulated depreciation	£7,455

    (iv) Computer – 33⅓ % straight line

        £2,850 × 33⅓ % = £950

Debit	Computer depreciation charge	£950
Credit	Computer accumulated depreciation	£950

(b) Rates of £500 are to be accrued

Debit	Rates	£500
Credit	Accruals	£500

(c) The insurance account includes an amount of £300 prepaid

Debit	Prepayments	£300
Credit	Insurance	£300

(d) An irrecoverable debt of £240 is to be written off

Debit	Irrecoverable debts expense	£240
Credit	Sales ledger control	£240

(e)   An allowance for 2% of the remaining receivables (debtors) is to be made

Allowance required 2% × (£15,240 – 240)   = £300
Balance on allowance account at start of the year   = £220
Increase in allowance required £300 – 220   = £80

Debit	Allowance for doubtful debts adjustment	£80
Credit	Allowance for doubtful debts	£80

(f)   Closing inventory at 31 March 20X4 has been valued at £5,200

Debit	Inventory account – statement of financial position	£5,200
Credit	Inventory account – statement of profit or loss	£5,200

In the adjustment column of the ETB the entries to make are both a debit and a credit entry against the opening inventory line with the value of the closing inventory.

At this stage you have completed the adjustments. Therefore to check that all of the adjustments have consisted of complete double entry you should total the debit and credit adjustment columns – they should be equal.

Account name	Ledger balances DR £	Ledger balances CR £	Adjustments DR £	Adjustments CR £	SPL DR £	SPL CR £	SFP DR £	SFP CR £
Buildings at cost	100,000							
Furniture and fittings at cost	4,800							
Motor vehicles at cost	32,700							
Computer at cost	2,850							
Accumulated depreciation at 1 April 20X3:								
– buildings		4,000		2,000				
– furniture and fittings		1,920		960				
– motor vehicles		7,850		7,455				
– computer		950		950				
Inventory at 1 April 20X3	4,400		5,200	5,200				
Bank	3,960							
Petty cash	100							
Sales ledger control	15,240			240				
Purchases ledger control		5,010						
Capital		130,000						
Sales revenue		155,020						
Sales returns	2,100							
Purchases	80,200							
Purchases returns		1,400	100					
Bank charges	200							
Discounts allowed	890		170					
Discounts received		1,260						
Wages	32,780							
Rates	5,500		500					
Telephone	1,140							
Electricity	1,480							
Insurance	1,500			300				
Motor expenses	1,580			200				
Office expenses	960		200					
Allowance for doubtful debts at 1 April 20X3		220		80				
Loan		820						
Drawings	15,800							
Suspense account	270			100 +170				
Buildings depreciation charge			2,000					
Furniture depreciation charge			960					
Motor vehicles depreciation charge			7,455					
Computer depreciation charge			950					
Accruals				500				
Prepayments			300					

Account name	Ledger balances		Adjustments		SPL		SFP	
	DR £	CR £	DR £	CR £	DR £	CR £	DR £	CR £
Irrecoverable debts expense			240					
Allowance for doubtful debts adjustment			80					
	308,450	308,450	18,155	18,155				

Step 4   Total and extend each line of the ETB into the statement of profit or loss or statement of financial position columns as appropriate.

The approach here is to take each line in turn and firstly add it across, then decide whether this is a statement of profit or loss balance or a statement of financial position balance. As examples:

- The buildings at cost account has a debit balance of £100,000 in the ledger balances column – there are no entries in the adjustment column so the only decision to make is whether this £100,000 is a debit in the statement of profit or loss or the statement of financial position – it is of course a non-current asset that will appear in the debit column in the statement of financial position.

- The accumulated depreciation for buildings has a credit of £4,000 in the ledger balance column and a further credit of £2,000 in the adjustment column – this totals to a credit of £6,000. This is the accumulated depreciation and therefore it is a statement of financial position figure – this £6,000 is therefore taken across to the credit column of the statement of financial position.

- Inventory is a complicated one – there are three figures that need to be extended across:

  - Opening inventory of £4,400 (the debit balance in the ledger balances column) is taken to the debit of the statement of profit or loss

  - The debit in the adjustment column is taken as a debit to the statement of financial position, being the closing inventory current asset

  - The credit in the adjustment column is taken as a credit in the statement of profit or loss, being the reduction in purchases cost in the cost of sales

- The sales ledger control account has a debit balance in the ledger balances column of £15,240 and a credit of £240 in the adjustment column – therefore the credit of £240 is deducted

from the debit of £15,240 to give a debit total of £15,000 which is taken to the debit column of the statement of financial position.

- The suspense account has a debit of £270 in the ledger balances column – there are two credit entries in the adjustment column which total to £270 therefore meaning that there is no balance to be extended across.

- The credit entry for accruals and the debit entry for prepayments are both taken across to the statement of financial position.

Now work carefully through the fully extended ETB ensuring that you are happy with each total and that you understand why the balances appear in the statement of profit or loss columns or the statement of financial position columns.

Remember:

Statement of profit or loss	–	Income
	–	Expenses
Statement of financial position	–	Assets
	–	Liabilities
	–	Capital

Account name	Ledger balances DR £	CR £	Adjustments DR £	CR £	SPL DR £	CR £	SFP DR £	CR £
Buildings at cost	100,000						100,000	
Furniture and fittings at cost	4,800						4,800	
Motor vehicles at cost	32,700						32,700	
Computer at cost	2,850						2,850	
Accumulated depreciation at 1 April 20X3:								
– buildings		4,000		2,000				6,000
– furniture and fittings		1,920		960				2,880
– motor vehicles		7,850		7,455				15,305
– computer		950		950				1,900
Inventory at 1 April 20X3	4,400		5,200	5,200	4,400	5,200	5,200	
Bank/cash	3,960						3,960	
Petty cash	100						100	
Sales ledger control	15,240			240			15,000	
Purchases ledger control		5,010						5,010
Capital		130,000						130,000
Sales revenue		155,020				155,020		
Sales returns	2,100				2,100			
Purchases	80,200				80,200			
Purchases returns		1,400	100			1,300		
Bank charges	200				200			
Discounts allowed	890		170		1,060			
Discounts received		1,260				1,260		
Wages	32,780				32,780			
Rates	5,500		500		6,000			
Telephone	1,140				1,140			
Electricity	1,480				1,480			
Insurance	1,500			300	1,200			
Motor expenses	1,580			200	1,380			
Office expenses	960		200		1,160			
Allowance for doubtful debts at 1 April 20X3		220		80				300
Loan		820						820
Drawings	15,800						15,800	
Suspense account	270			100 +170				
Buildings depreciation charge			2,000		2,000			
Furniture depreciation charge			960		960			
Motor vehicles depreciation charge			7,455		7,455			
Computer depreciation charge			950		950			
Accruals				500				500
Prepayments			300				300	
Irrecoverable debts expense			240		240			
Allowance for doubtful debts adjustment			80		80			
	308,450	308,450	18,155	18,155				

Step 5   Total the statement of profit or loss columns to find the profit or loss for the year:

- If the credits in the statement of profit of loss exceed the debits then there is more income than expense, so a profit has been made. This is the balancing debit in the statement of profit or loss and it requires a new account line of profit/loss. This same figure is also a credit in the statement of financial position columns (because it is adding to the owner's capital, which is always a credit balance).

- If the debits in the statement of profit or loss exceed the credits then there are more expenses than income and a loss has been made. This is the balancing credit in the statement of profit or loss (again this uses the new account line of profit/loss). This same figure is entered as a debit in the statement of financial position columns (because it is reducing the owner's capital).

Total the statement of financial position columns – they should be equal.

Account name	Ledger balance DR £	Ledger balance CR £	Adjustments DR £	Adjustments CR £	Statement of profit or loss DR £	Statement of profit or loss CR £	Statement of financial position DR £	Statement of financial position CR £
Building at cost	100,000						100,000	
Furniture and fittings at cost	4,800						4,800	
Motor vehicles at cost	32,700						32,700	
Computer at cost	2,850						2,850	
Accumulated depreciation at 1 April 2013:								
– buildings		4,000		2,000				6,000
– furniture and fittings		1,920		960				2,880
– motor vehicles		7,850		7,455				15,305
– computer		950		950				1,900
Stock (inventory) at 1 April 20X3	4,400		5,200	5,200	4,400	5,200	5,200	
Bank	3,960						3,960	
Petty cash	100						100	
Sales ledger control	15,240			240			15,000	
Purchases ledger control		5,010						5,010
Capital		130,000						130,000
Sales revenue		155,020				155,020		
Sales return	2,100				2,100			
Purchases	80,000				80,000			
Purchases returns		1,400	100			1,300		
Bank charges	200				200			

Account name	Ledger balance DR £	Ledger balance CR £	Adjustments DR £	Adjustments CR £	Statement of profit or loss DR £	Statement of profit or loss CR £	Statement of financial position DR £	Statement of financial position CR £
Discounts allowed	890		170		1,060			
Discounts received		1,260				1,260		
Wages	32,780				32,780			
Rates	5,500		500		6,000			
Telephone	1,140				1,140			
Electricity	1,480				1,480			
Insurance	1,500			300	1,200			
Motor expenses	1,580			200	1,380			
Office expenses	960		200		1,160			
Allowance for doubtful debts at 1 April 20X3		220		80				300
Loan		820						820
Drawings	15,800						15,800	
Suspense account	270			100 / 170				
Buildings depreciation charge			2,000		2,000			
Furniture depreciation charge			960		960			
Motor vehicles depreciation charge			7,455		7,455			
Computer depreciation charge			950		950			
Accruals				500				500
Prepayments			300				300	
Irrecoverable debts expense			240		240			
Allowance for doubtful debts adjustment			80		80			
Profit/loss					17,995			17,995
	308,450	308,450	18,155	18,155	162,780	162,780	180,710	180,710

In this case a profit of £17,995 was made. This is the balancing figure in the statement of profit or loss columns and is shown as a credit in the statement of financial position, to be added to the capital for the period.

Once it is entered into the credit column in the statement of financial position the statement of financial position columns should be totalled and the two column totals should be equal.

Task 1

If the credit balances exceed the debit balances in the statement of profit or loss columns this means the business has made a profit/loss for the period. The other entry to be made with this balancing amount is in the debit column/credit column of the statement of financial position.

DISPOSALS AND THE ETB

When a business disposes of a non-current asset and a profit or loss on disposal arises, the ETB can be used to process the journals necessary for this, calculate the profit or loss on disposal and allocate it correctly in the statement of profit or loss columns.

HOW IT WORKS

Adam Singleton operates a very simple business and his trial balance as at 31 December is as follows:

Ledger account	Debit £	Credit £
Capital		5,000
Sales revenue		15,000
Purchases	7,000	
Sales ledger control	6,000	
Purchases ledger control		2,000
Bank/cash	5,000	
Machine at cost	10,000	
Machine accumulated depreciation		6,000
	28,000	28,000

After the extraction of the trial balance on 31 December Adam disposed of the machine in return for a cheque for £3,500.

We need to adjust for this transaction and extend the ETB to arrive at Adam's profit for the period.

Step 1   Prepare journal entries for the disposal:

Account name	Amount £	Debit (✓)	Credit (✓)
Disposals	10,000	✓	
Machine at cost	10,000		✓
Machine accumulated depreciation	6,000	✓	
Disposals	6,000		✓
Bank/cash	3,500	✓	
Disposals	3,500		✓

Step 2   Next we process these adjustments on the ETB:

Extended trial balance as at 31 December

	Ledger balances DR £	Ledger balances CR £	Adjustments DR £	Adjustments CR £	SPL DR £	SPL CR £	SFP DR £	SFP CR £
Capital		5,000						
Sales revenue		15,000						
Purchases	7,000							
Sales ledger control	6,000							
Purchases ledger control		2,000						
Bank/cash	5,000		3,500					
Machine at cost	10,000			10,000				
Machine acc depreciation		6,000	6,000					
Disposals			10,000	6,000				
				3,500				
	28,000	28,000	19,500	19,500				

Step 3   Debits exceed credits by £500 on the disposal line of the ETB, so we know that the disposal has been at a £500 loss. This amount is entered in the debit column of the statement of profit or loss, so the disposals line now cross casts.

Extended trial balance as at 31 December

	Ledger balances DR £	Ledger balances CR £	Adjustments DR £	Adjustments CR £	SPL DR £	SPL CR £	SFP DR £	SFP CR £
Capital		5,000						
Sales revenue		15,000						
Purchases	7,000							
Sales ledger control	6,000							
Purchases ledger control		2,000						
Bank/cash	5,000		3,500					
Machine at cost	10,000			10,000				
Machine acc depreciation		6,000	6,000					
Disposals			10,000	6,000 3,500	500			
Profit								
	28,000	28,000	19,500	19,500	500			

Step 4 The remainder of the balances are also extended, and the statement of profit or loss columns are totalled:

Extended trial balance as at 31 December

Ledger account	Ledger balances DR £	Ledger balances CR £	Adjustments DR £	Adjustments CR £	SPL DR £	SPL CR £	SFP DR £	SFP CR £
Capital		5,000						5,000
Sales revenue		15,000				15,000		
Purchases	7,000				7,000			
Sales ledger control	6,000						6,000	
Purchases ledger control		2,000						2,000
Bank/cash	5,000		3,500				8,500	
Machine at cost	10,000			10,000				
Machine acc depreciation		6,000	6,000					
Disposals			10,000	6,000 3,500	500			
Profit								
	28,000	8,000	19,500	19,500	7,500	15,000		

Step 5   The profit for the year of £7,500 is entered on the debit side of the statement of profit or loss, to make it balance, and on the credit side of the statement of financial position, again to make it balance. The statement of profit or loss and statement of financial position columns are then totalled, and should balance.

Extended trial balance as at 31 December

	Ledger balances		Adjustments		SPL		SFP	
	DR £	CR £	DR £	CR £	DR £	CR £	DR £	CR £
Capital		5,000						5,000
Sales revenue		15,000				15,000		
Purchases	7,000				7,000			
Sales ledger control	6,000						6,000	
Purchases ledger control		2,000						2,000
Bank/cash	5,000		3,500				8,500	
Machine at cost	10,000			10,000				
Machine acc dep		6,000	6,000					
Disposals			10,000	6,000	500			
				3,500				
Profit					7,500			7,500
	28,000	28,000	19,500	19,500	15,000	15,000	14,500	14,500

Task 2

The following balances have been taken from the trial balance of XYZ. Rent paid £1,800, capital £15,000, purchases £10,000, sales revenue £12,000, wages £5,000, sundry expenses £1,000, cash £9,200. What is the trial balance total on the debit side?

A   £26,000

B   £29,000

C   £42,000

D   £27,000

Task 3

A suspense account shows a credit balance of £130. This could be due to:

A   Omitting a sale of £130 from the sales ledger

B   Recording a purchase of £130 twice in the purchases account

C   Failing to write off an irrecoverable debt of £130

D   Recording an electricity bill paid of £65 by debiting the bank account and crediting the electricity account

CHAPTER OVERVIEW

- Once the initial trial balance has been prepared any errors that have caused a suspense account and any year end adjustments are put through the accounts in order to arrive at the figures for the final accounts – this can all be done in the extended trial balance

- The first stage is to enter all of the ledger account balances into the ETB and to check that it balances – if it does not balance then a suspense account is entered in order to create a balanced trial balance

- The suspense account is then cleared by entering the correcting entries in the adjustments columns of the ETB

- Any year end adjustments are then also entered in the adjustment columns for depreciation, irrecoverable and doubtful debts and accruals and prepayments

- The closing inventory figure is entered as a debit and a credit entry in the adjustment columns on the inventory line

- Each line of the ETB is then totalled and extended into either the statement of profit or loss columns or the statement of financial position columns as a debit or a credit – in the statement of profit or loss there are income and expenses – in the statement of financial position there are assets, liabilities and capital

- The statement of profit or loss columns are then totalled and the balancing figure is inserted as a new account line, the profit/loss, which is also inserted in the statement of financial position columns – a debit in the statement of profit or loss column is a credit in the statement of financial position column and vice versa

- The final stage is to total the statement of financial position columns and these should now agree

Keyword

Extended trial balance – an accounting technique of moving from the trial balance, through the year end adjustments to the figures for the final accounts

TEST YOUR LEARNING

Test 1

When preparing an extended trial balance what do you do if you discover that the initial trial balance does not balance?

Test 2

What entries if any are made in the adjustments column for the closing inventory?

Both a debit and a credit

A debit

A credit

No entry

Test 3

The closing inventory figure is a debit entry/credit entry in the statement of profit or loss columns and a debit entry/credit entry in the statement of financial position columns of the ETB.

ANSWERS TO CHAPTER TASKS

CHAPTER 1 Accounting principles

1 a receivable

2 a credit note

3 the purchases day book

4 the purchases ledger

5

Sales ledger control account

Date	Details	Amount £	Date	Details	Amount £
4 Mar	Sales revenue	2,400			

Sales revenue

Date	Details	Amount £	Date	Details	Amount £
			4 Mar	Receivables	2,400

Purchases

Date	Details	Amount £	Date	Details	Amount £
4 Mar	Payables	1,800			

Purchases ledger control account

Date	Details	Amount £	Date	Details	Amount £
			4 Mar	Purchases	1,800

Phone

Date	Details	Amount £	Date	Details	Amount £
4 Mar	Bank/cash	140			

Bank/cash

Date	Details	Cash £	Bank £	Date	Details	Cash £	Bank £
				4 Mar	Phone		140
				4 Mar	Drawings		500

Drawings

Date	Details	Amount £	Date	Details	Amount £
4 Mar	Bank/cash	500			

6

Sales ledger control account

Date	Details	Amount £	Date	Details	Amount £
17 Feb	Sales revenue	900	25 Feb	Bank/cash	700
			28 Feb	Bal c/d	200
	Total	900		Total	900
1 Mar	Bal b/d	200			

7   The correct answer is **B**.

If the bookkeeping has been accurate, the total of the debits will equal the total of the credits in the trial balance.

CHAPTER 2 **Accounting concepts**

1

	£	Description
Rent	480	Expense
Motor van	7,400	Asset
Payables	1,900	Liability
Heat and light	210	Expense
Discounts received	50	Income
Motor expenses	310	Expense
Sales revenue	40,800	Income
Opening inventory	2,100	Asset
Loan	2,000	Liability
Stationery	330	Expense
Capital	7,980	Capital
Phone	640	Expense
Discount allowed	60	Expense
Purchases	22,600	Expense
Receivables	3,400	Asset
Wages	9,700	Expense
Drawings	4,000	Reduction of capital
Office cleaning	220	Expense
Travel and accommodation	660	Expense
Bank	483	Asset
Cash	137	Asset

2

	£	£
Sales revenue		136,700
Less cost of sales		
Opening inventory	11,300	
Purchases	97,500	
	108,800	
Less closing inventory	(10,600)	
		98,200
Gross profit		38,500

3

	Debit	Credit	Statement of profit or loss	Statement of financial position
	£	£		
Rent	480		✓	
Motor van	7,400			✓
Payables		1,900		✓
Heat and light	210		✓	
Discounts received		50	✓	
Motor expenses	310		✓	
Sales revenue		40,800	✓	
Opening inventory	2,100		✓	
Loan		2,000		✓
Stationery	330		✓	
Capital		7,980		✓
Phone	640		✓	
Discount allowed	60		✓	
Purchases	22,600		✓	
Receivables	3,400			✓
Wages	9,700		✓	
Drawings	4,000			✓
Office cleaning	220		✓	
Travel and accommodation	660		✓	
Bank	483			✓
Cash	137			✓
	52,730	52,730		

4   Accruals

CHAPTER 3 **Purchase of non-current assets**

1   Capital expenditure £15,000

Revenue expenditure £4,000

Expenditure on Machine A is capital expenditure as it is a major improvement of the asset. The £4,000 repair costs of Machine B is revenue expenditure as this is just the running costs of the machine.

2

Machinery account

	£		£
Purchases ledger control	17,000		
Wages	1,400		

Purchases ledger control account

	£		£
		Machinery	17,000

Wages account

	£		£
		Machinery	1,400

3

Account	Amount £	Debit	Credit
Motor vehicles	78,800	✓	
Motor expenses	800	✓	
Bank account	79,600		✓

4

Account name	Amount £	Debit	Credit
Motor vehicles	25,000	✓	
Bank / cash	15,000		✓
Disposals	10,000		✓
Being the purchase of a new car for cash/part exchange.			

CHAPTER 4 Depreciation of non-current assets

1   Carrying amount = Cost – depreciation to date

Carrying amount = £8,000 – £3,000 = £5,000

2   Depreciation charge $= \dfrac{£22,000 - 9,000}{4}$

= £3,250 per annum

Carrying amount   = £22,000 – (2 × 3,250) = £15,500

3

	£
Original cost	22,000
Year 1 depreciation 22,000 × 20%	(4,400)
Carrying amount at end of year 1	17,600
Year 2 depreciation 17,600 × 20%	(3,520)
Carrying amount at end of year 2	14,080
Year 3 depreciation 14,080 × 20%	(2,816)
Carrying amount at end of year 3	11,264
Year 4 depreciation 11,264 × 20%	(2,253)
Carrying amount	9,011

4

Depreciation charge

	£		£
Accumulated depreciation	24,000		

Accumulated depreciation

	£		£
		Depreciation charge	24,000

Statement of profit or loss

Expenses:	£
Depreciation charge	24,000

SFP

Non-current assets:

	Cost	Depreciation	Carrying amount
	£	£	£
Machinery	120,000	24,000	96,000

5   False

The diminishing balance method results in larger amounts being charged in earlier years and smaller amounts in subsequent years.

CHAPTER 5 **Disposal of non-current assets**

1

(a)

	£
Original cost	11,200
20X7 depreciation 11,200 × 30%	3,360
Carrying amount 31 Dec 20X7	7,840
20X8 depreciation 7,840 × 30%	2,352
Carrying amount 31 Dec 20X8	5,488

(b)

	£
Carrying amount at 31 December 20X8	5,488
Disposal proceeds	5,000
Loss on disposal	488

(c)

Motor car at cost account

	£		£
1 Jan 20X7 Bank	11,200	31 Dec 20X8 Disposal	11,200

Accumulated depreciation on the motor car account

	£		£
31 Dec 20X7 Balance c/d	3,360	31 Dec 20X7 Depreciation	3,360
31 Dec 20X8 Disposal	5,712	1 Jan 20X8 Balance b/d	3,360
		31 Dec 20X8 Depreciation	2,352
	5,712		5,712

Disposals account

	£		£
31 Dec 20X8 Motor car at cost	11,200	31 Dec 20X8 Motor car accumulated depreciation	5,712
		31 Dec 20X8 Proceeds	5,000
		31 Dec 20X8 SPL – loss	488
	11,200		11,200

2

Car at cost account

	£		£
1 Mar 20X6 Bank/cash	10,000	31 May 20X8 Disposals	10,000
31 May 20X8 Bank/cash	6,200	31 May 20X8 Balance c/d	11,000
31 May 20X8 Disposals	4,800		
	21,000		21,000
1 June 20X8 Balance b/d	11,000		

Car accumulated depreciation account

	£		£
31 May 20X8 Disposals	5,500	31 May 20X8 Balance b/d	5,500

Disposals account

	£		£
31 May 20X8 Car at cost	10,000	31 May 20X8 Car accumulated depreciation	5,500
31 May 20X8 SPL – profit on disposal	300	31 May 20X8 Car at cost	4,800
	10,300		10,300

3

Non-Current Asset Register

Non-current asset number	24116
Description	Fork lift truck XC355
Location	Warehouse
Supplier	Leyland Machinery

Date	Cost £	Expected life (years)	Estimated residual value £	Depreciation method	Depreciation rate	Depreciation charge for the year £	Acc dep at end of the year £	Carrying amount at end of year £	Disposal proceeds £	Profit or loss on disposal £
20X5										
1 May	34,000	4	6,250	Reducing balance	30%					
31 Dec						10,200	10,200	23,800		
20X6										
31 Dec						7,140	17,340	16,660		
20X7										
31 Dec						4,998	22,338	11,662		
20X8										
20 Mar									10,500	(1,162)

4   The correct answer is **D**.

CHAPTER 6 Accruals and prepayments

1   This will | increase | phone expenses in the old accounting year, and it will be shown as | a liability | on the statement of financial position at the year end.

2

Phone account

	£		£
31 Dec Balance b/d	2,600		
31 Dec Accrual c/d	480	31 Dec Statement of profit or loss	3,080
	3,080		3,080
		1 Jan Accrual b/d	480

3

Rent account

	£		£
31 Dec Balance b/d	3,200	31 Dec Statement of profit or loss	2,900
		31 Dec Prepayment c/d (£900 × 1/3)	300
	3,200		3,200
1 Jan Prepayment b/d	300		

4   Asset

Accrued income is due but has not been received, therefore it is a form of asset.

CHAPTER 7 **Inventory**

1   Cost   =   £13.80

Net realisable value   =   £14.00 – 0.50

=   £13.50

Each unit should be valued at £13.50, the lower of cost and net realisable value

2   12 May – sale – 70 units @ £3.50

30 May – sale – 80 units   30 units @ £3.50

50 units @ £4.00

Closing inventory – 50 units @ £4.00 = £200.00

3   The purchases account.

The cost of goods purchased should **never** be debited to the inventory account. The inventory account is adjusted at the end of the accounting period only.

CHAPTER 8　Irrecoverable debts and doubtful debts

1

Account name	Debit £	Credit £
Irrecoverable debts expense	976	
Sales ledger control		976
Being the write-off of a specific receivable		

2

Account name	Debit £	Credit £
Bank/cash account	1,000	
Irrecoverable debts expense account		1,000
Being the recovery of a specific receivable previously written-off		

3

Account name	Debit £	Credit £
Irrecoverable debts expense	680	
Sales ledger control		680
Allowance for doubtful debts adjustment	630	
Allowance for doubtful debts		630
Being the write-off of one debt and the set-up of a new general allowance for doubtful debts		

4

Account name	Debit £	Credit £
Irrecoverable debts expense	2,400	
Sales ledger control		2,400
Allowance for doubtful debts	924	
Allowance for doubtful debts adjustment		924
Being write-off of irrecoverable debt and reduction of allowance for doubtful debts from £1,500 to ((£60,000 − £2,400) × 1%) = £576		

5

Account name	Debit £	Credit £
Allowance for doubtful debts (SFP)	√	
Allowance for doubtful debts adj (SPL)		√

6　Prudence

CHAPTER 9   **Bank reconciliations**

1   £12,255

Workings	Debit	Credit
	£	£
Balance per cash book	12,450	
Standing order for rent		400
BGC receipt from customer	230	
Bank charges		25
Adjusted cash book balance c/d		12,255
	12,680	12,680

2

Account name	Amount	Debit	Credit
	£	(✓)	(✓)
Sales ledger control account	500	√	
Cash book	500		√

3   The correct answer is **C**.

CHAPTER 10   **Control account reconciliations**

1

Account name	Debit £	Credit £
Purchases ledger control	500	
Sales ledger control		500

Being the setting off of sales ledger and purchases ledger balances

2   The sales ledger control account but not the individual balances in the sales ledger.

3

Adjustment	Amount £	Debit (✓)	Credit (✓)
Sales ledger control	120		✓

The other side of the entry would be a debit to the discounts allowed account.

4

Adjustment	Amount £	Debit (✓)	Credit (✓)
Purchases ledger balances	700		✓

5   The correct answer is **D**.

6   The correct answer is **B**.

CHAPTER 11 **The trial balance, errors and the suspense account**

1   (a) Debit   Purchases returns
          Credit   Statement of profit or loss

     (b) Debit   Statement of profit or loss
          Credit   Insurance

     (c) No adjustment required as this is a statement of financial position item.

2   The correct answer is **A**.

3   The correct answer is **A**.

CHAPTER 12 **The extended trial balance**

1 This means that the business has made a **profit** for the period and the other entry is in the **credit column** of the statement of financial position.

2 The correct answer is **D.**

   Workings:

	DR £	CR £
Rent	1,800	
Capital		15,000
Purchases	10,000	
Sales revenue		12,000
Wages	5,000	
Sundry expenses	1,000	
Cash	9,200	
	27,000	27,000

3 The correct answer is **B.**

   £130 will be debited twice to purchases, giving rise to a credit balance in the suspense account.

TEST YOUR LEARNING – ANSWERS

CHAPTER 1 Accounting principles

1

Bank account

Date	Details	£	Date	Details	£
1/3	Capital	20,000	1/3	Furn & fit	3,200
10/3	Sales revenue	1,800	4/3	Purchases	4,400
24/3	Receivables	3,500	6/3	Rent	600
			28/3	Drawings	1,000
			30/3	Payables	1,800
			31/3	Wages	900
			31/3	Balance c/d	13,400
		25,300			25,300
1/4	Balance b/d	13,400			

Capital account

Date	Details	£	Date	Details	£
			1/3	Bank/cash	20,000

Furniture and fittings account

Date	Details	£	Date	Details	£
1/3	Bank/cash	3,200			

Purchases account

Date	Details	£	Date	Details	£
4/3	Bank/cash	4,400	31/3	Balance c/d	7,100
20/3	Payables	2,700			
		7,100			7,100
1/4	Balance b/d	7,100			

Rent account

Date	Details	£	Date	Details	£
6/3	Bank/cash	600			

Sales revenue account

Date	Details	£	Date	Details	£
31/3	Balance c/d	8,300	10/3	Bank/cash	1,800
			15/3	Receivables	4,900
			29/3	Receivables	1,600
		8,300			8,300
			1/4	Balance b/d	8,300

Sales ledger control account

Date	Details	£	Date	Details	£
15/3	Sales revenue	4,900	24/3	Bank/cash	3,500
29/3	Sales revenue	1,600	31/3	Balance c/d	3,000
		6,500			6,500
1/4	Balance b/d	3,000			

Purchases ledger control account

Date	Details	£	Date	Details	£
30/3	Bank/cash	1,800	20/3	Purchases	2,700
31/3	Balance c/d	900			
		2,700			2,700
			1/4	Balance b/d	900

Drawings account

Date	Details	£	Date	Details	£
28/3	Bank/cash	1,000			

Wages account

Date	Details	£	Date	Details	£
31/3	Bank/cash	900			

Trial balance as at 31 March

	Debit £	Credit £
Bank	13,400	
Capital		20,000
Furniture and fittings	3,200	
Purchases	7,100	
Rent	600	
Sales revenue		8,300
Receivables	3,000	
Payables		900
Drawings	1,000	
Wages	900	
	29,000	29,000

2 General ledger

Sales ledger control account

Date	Details	£	Date	Details	£
31 Mar	SDB	1,390	31 Mar	SRDB	60
			31 Mar	CRB	720
			31 Mar	CRB - discounts	10
			31 Mar	Balance c/d	600
		1,390			1,390
1 Apr	Balance b/d	600			

Sales revenue account

Date	Details	£	Date	Details	£
			31 Mar	SDB	1,390
31 Mar	Balance c/d	3,060	31 Mar	CRB	1,670
		3,060			3,060
			1 Apr	Balance b/d	3,060

Sales returns account

Date	Details	£	Date	Details	£
31 Mar	SRDB	60			

Purchases ledger control account

Date	Details	£	Date	Details	£
31 Mar	PRDB	80	31 Mar	PDB	1,400
31 Mar	CPB	870			
31 Mar	CPB – discounts	40			
31 Mar	Balance c/d	410			
		1,400			1,400
			1 Apr	Balance b/d	410

Purchases account

Date	Details	£	Date	Details	£
31 Mar	PDB	1,400			
31 Mar	CPB	2,250	31 Mar	Balance c/d	3,650
		3,650			3,650
1 Apr	Balance b/d	3,650			

Purchases returns account

Date	Details	£	Date	Details	£
			31 Mar	PRDB	80

Capital account

Date	Details	£	Date	Details	£
			31 Mar	CRB	15,000

Discounts allowed account

Date	Details	£	Date	Details	£
31 Mar	CRB	10			

Wages account

Date	Details	£	Date	Details	£
31 Mar	CPB	2,200			

Shop fittings account

Date	Details	£	Date	Details	£
31 Mar	CPB	1,100			

Discounts received account

Date	Details	£	Date	Details	£
			31 Mar	CPB	40

Bank/cash

Date	Details	£	Date	Details	£
31 Mar	CRB	17,390	31 Mar	CPB	6,420
			31 Mar	Balance c/d	10,970
		17,390			17,390
1 Apr	Balance b/d	10,970			

Sales ledger

J Simpson

Date	Details	£	Date	Details	£
4 Mar	SDB 0001	420	20 Mar	CRB	420

F Barnet

Date	Details	£	Date	Details	£
12 Mar	SDB 0002	350	19 Mar	SRDB CN 001	40
			31 Mar	CRB	300
			31 Mar	CRB – discount	10
		350			350

H Jerry

Date	Details	£	Date	Details	£
18 Mar	SDB 0003	180	25 Mar	SRDB CN 002	20
			31 Mar	Balance c/d	160
		180			180
1 Apr	Balance b/d	160			

D Dawson

Date	Details	£	Date	Details	£
28 Mar	SDB 0004	440			

Purchases ledger

L Lilley

Date	Details	£	Date	Details	£
12 Mar	CPB 0003	560	1 Mar	PDB 89432	590
12 Mar	CPD – discounts	30			
		590			590

O Rools

Date	Details	£	Date	Details	£
10 Mar	PRDB C357	80	7 Mar	PDB 12332	400
20 Mar	CPB	310			
20 Mar	CPB – discounts	10			
		400			400

R Terry

Date	Details	£	Date	Details	£
			24 Mar	PDB 0532	410

Trial balance as at 31 March

	Debit £	Credit £
Receivables	600	
Sales revenue		3,060
Sales returns	60	
Payables		410
Purchases	3,650	
Purchases returns		80
Capital		15,000
Discounts allowed	10	
Wages	2,200	
Shop fittings	1,100	
Discounts received		40
Bank/cash	10,970	
	18,590	18,590

CHAPTER 2   **Accounting concepts**

1

	Debit £	Credit £	Type of balance	SPL or SFP
Sales revenue		41,200	Income	SPL
Loan		1,500	Liability	SFP
Wages	7,000		Expense	SPL
Non-current assets	7,100		Asset	SFP
Opening inventory	1,800		Expense (see note)	SPL
Receivables	3,400		Asset	SFP
Discounts received		40	Income	SPL
Postage	100		Expense	SPL
Bank	300		Asset	SFP
Capital		9,530	Capital	SFP
Rent	500		Expense	SPL
Purchases	30,100		Expense	SPL
Payables		2,500	Liability	SFP
Discounts allowed	70		Expense	SPL
Drawings	3,000		Reduction of capital	SFP
Electricity	800		Expense	SPL
Telephone	600		Expense	SPL
	54,770	54,770		

Note   Opening inventory is included in the statement of profit or loss as part of the calculation of cost of sales. It is the closing inventory balance, which is an asset at the end of the accounting period, that is included in the statement of financial position.

2   (a)   The gross profit of a business is the profit from the **trading activities**.

     (b)   The total of the current assets minus the current liabilities is known as **net current assets**.

3   (a)   Accruals concept

     (b)   Going concern concept

     (c)   Materiality concept

CHAPTER 3   **Purchase of non-current assets**

1 (a) Capital expenditure   £15,700
        Revenue expenditure   £100

   (b) Capital expenditure   £61,100

   (c) Capital expenditure   £68,600
        Revenue expenditure   £800

2

	Account	Amount	Debit	Credit
		£		
(a)	Furniture and fittings	4,200	✓	
	Bank/cash	4,200		✓
	Being purchase of desks and chairs for head office			
(b)	Computers	2,300	✓	
	Computer expenses	100	✓	
	Purchases ledger control	2,400		✓
	Being purchase of computer and rewritable CDs			
(c)	Machinery	10,600	✓	
	Purchases	200		✓
	Wages	800		✓
	Bank/cash	9,600		✓
	Being purchase and installation of machine			

3   On the date of payment of the deposit

CHAPTER 4   **Depreciation of non-current assets**

1   The main accounting concept underlying the depreciation of non-current assets is the ⌐accruals⌐ concept.

2   Depreciation charge $= \dfrac{£11,500 - 2,500}{5 \text{ years}} = £1,800$ per annum

Carrying amount at 31 December 20X8 $= £11,500 - (2 \times £1,800) = £7,900$

3

	£
Original cost	16,400
Depreciation to 31 Dec 20X7 (16,400 × 35%)	5,740
Carrying amount at 31 Dec 20X7	10,660
Depreciation to 31 Dec 20X8 (10,660 × 35%)	3,731
Carrying amount at 31 Dec 20X8	6,929

4   Depreciation charge $=$ (£240,000 – £135,000) × 30%

$=$ £31,500

5   Depreciation charge $=$ £24,000 × 20% × 7/12

$=$ £2,800

CHAPTER 5   Disposal of non-current assets

1 (a)

		£
Original cost		2,200
20X5 depreciation 2,200 × 40%		880
20X5 carrying amount		1,320
20X6 depreciation 1,320 × 40%		528
20X6 carrying amount		792
20X7 depreciation 792 × 40%		317
20X7 carrying amount		475
Disposal proceeds		200
Loss on disposal		275

(b)

Computer at cost account

Date	Details	£	Date	Details	£
1 April 20X5	Bank	2,200	14 May 20X8	Disposal	2,200

Computer accumulated depreciation account

Date	Details	£	Date	Details	£
31 Dec 20X5	Balance c/d	880	31 Dec 20X5	Expense	880
			1 Jan 20X6	Balance b/d	880
31 Dec 20X6	Balance c/d	1,408	31 Dec 20X6	Expense	528
		1,408			1,408
			1 Jan 20X7	Balance b/d	1,408
31 Dec 20X7	Balance c/d	1,725	31 Dec 20X7	Expense	317
		1,725			1,725
14 May 20X8	Disposal	1,725	1 Jan 20X8	Balance b/d	1,725

Disposals account

Date	Details	£	Date	Details	£
14 May 20X8	Cost	2,200	14 May 20X8	Depreciation	1,725
			14 May 20X8	Proceeds	200
			14 May 20X8	SPL – loss	275
		2,200			2,200

2 (a)

	£
Original cost	7,200
20X6 depreciation 7,200 × 25% × 2/12	(300)
20X7 depreciation 7,200 × 25%	(1,800)
20X8 depreciation 7,200 × 25% × 8/12	(1,200)
Carrying amount 31 July 20X8	3,900
Proceeds	(3,800)
Loss on disposal	100

(b)

Machine at cost account

Date	Details	£	Date	Details	£
1 Oct 20X6	Bank	7,200	31 July 20X8	Disposal	7,200

Machine accumulated depreciation account

Date	Details	£	Date	Details	£
30 Nov 20X6	Balance c/d	300	30 Nov 20X6	Expense	300
			1 Dec 20X6	Balance b/d	300
30 Nov 20X7	Balance c/d	2,100	30 Nov 20X7	Expense	1,800
		2,100			2,100
			1 Dec 20X7	Balance b/d	2,100
30 July 20X8	Disposal	3,300	31 July 20X8	Expense	1,200
		3,300			3,300

Disposals account

Date	Details	£	Date	Details	£
31 July 20X8	Cost	7,200	31 July 20X8	Depreciation	3,300
			31 July 20X8	Proceeds	3,800
			31 July 20X8	SPL – loss	100
		7,200			7,200

3   (a)   A loss on disposal can also be described as **under-depreciation**.

       (b)   A profit on disposal can also be described as **over-depreciation**.

4

Van at cost account

Date	Details	£	Date	Details	£
1 July 20X5	Bank	13,600	30 Apr 20X8	Disposal	13,600
30 Apr 20X8	Bank	12,200			
30 Apr 20X8	Disposal				
	(16,700 − 12,200)	4,500	30 Apr 20X8	Balance c/d	16,700
		30,300			30,300

Van accumulated depreciation account

Date	Details	£	Date	Details	£
30 Apr 20X8	Disposal	9,000	30 Apr 20X8	Balance b/d	9,000

Disposals account

Date	Details	£	Date	Details	£
30 Apr 20X8	Cost	13,600	30 Apr 20X8	Depreciation	9,000
			30 Apr 20X8	Cost	4,500
			30 Apr 20X8	SPL – loss	100
		13,600			13,600

5

NON-CURRENT ASSET REGISTER
Non-current asset number 10435
Description Computer 1036525
Location Sales Department
Supplier **Timing Company Ltd**

Date	Cost £	Expected life (years)	Estimated residual value £	Depreciation method	Depreciation rate	Depreciation charge for the year £	Acc dep at end of the year £	Carrying amount at end of year £	Disposal proceeds £	Profit or loss on disposal £
20X6 1 Mar	4,800	4	600	Reducing balance	40%					
31 July						1,920	1,920	2,880		
20X7 31 July						1,152	3,072	1,728		
20X8 27 Jun									700	(1,028)

280

CHAPTER 6   **Accruals and prepayments**

1   (a)   Rent paid in advance for the following accounting period would appear as **a prepayment** in the statement of financial position.

(b)   Motor expenses owing to the local garage would appear as **an accrual** in the statement of financial position.

2   (a)   In the statement of profit or loss the heat and light expense would be £**870**. In the statement of financial position there would be an **accrual** for £**200**.

(b)   In the statement of profit or loss the rental income would be £**340**. In the statement of financial position there would be a **prepayment of income** of £**40**.

(c)   In the statement of profit or loss the insurance expense would be £**1,100**. In the statement of financial position there would be a **prepayment** of £**300**.

(d)   In the statement of profit or loss commissions income would be £**200**. In the statement of financial position there would be an **accrual of income** of £**20**.

3

Motor expenses account

Date	Details	£	Date	Details	£
30 June	Balance b/d	845	30 June	Prepayments c/d (150 × 6/12)	75
			30 June	Statement of profit or loss	770
		845			845
1 July	Prepayments b/d	75			

4

Electricity account

Date	Details	£	Date	Details	£
31 Mar	Balance b/d	470	31 Mar	Statement of profit or loss	650
31 Mar	Accruals c/d	180			
		650			650
			1 Apr	Accruals b/d	180

CHAPTER 7 **Inventory**

1 (a) Cost   =   £25.80 + 1.00 = £26.80

NRV   =   £28.00 – 1.10 = £26.90

(b) 120 × £26.80 = £3,216.00

CHAPTER 8 Irrecoverable debts and doubtful debts

1 General ledger

Sales ledger control account

	£		£
Balance b/d	25,673	Irrecoverable debts expense	445
		(157 + 288)	
		Balance c/d	25,228
	25,673		25,673
Balance b/d	25,228		

Irrecoverable debts expense account

	£		£
Sales ledger control	445	Statement of profit or loss	445

Sales ledger

H Taylor

	£		£
Balance b/d	157	Irrecoverable debts expense	157

C Phelps

	£		£
Balance b/d	288	Irrecoverable debts expense	288

2

Bank account

	£		£
Irrecoverable debts expense account	250		

Irrecoverable debts expense account

	£		£
		Bank account	250

3 (a)

	£
Sales ledger control account	11,650
Irrecoverable debt	(350)
	11,300
Specific allowance	(200)
Remaining receivables (debtors)	11,100
General allowance 2% × £11,100	222
Specific allowance	200
Total allowance for doubtful debts	422

(b)

Irrecoverable debts expense account

	£		£
Sales ledger control account	350	Statement of profit or loss	350

Sales ledger control account

	£		£
Balance b/d	11,650	Irrecoverable debts expense	350
		Balance c/d	11,300
	11,650		11,650
Balance b/d	11,300		

Allowance for doubtful debts adjustment account

	£		£
Allowance for doubtful debts	422	Statement of profit or loss	422

Allowance for doubtful debts account

	£		£
		Allowance for doubtful debts adjustment account	422

4

Irrecoverable debts expense account

		£			£
20X7			20X7		
31 Dec	Sales ledger control	370	31 Dec	Statement of profit or loss	370
20X8			20X8		
31 Dec	Sales ledger control	400	31 Dec	Statement of profit or loss	400

Allowance for doubtful debts adjustment account

		£			£
20X7			20X7		
31 Dec	Allowance for doubtful debts	228	31 Dec	Statement of profit or loss	228
20X8			20X8		
31 Dec	Statement of profit or loss	168	31 Dec	Allowance for doubtful debts	168

Allowance for doubtful debts account

		£			£
20X7			20X7		
			1 Jan	Balance b/d	1,460
31 Dec	Balance c/d	1,688	31 Dec	Allowance for doubtful debts adjustment	228
		1,688			1,688
20X8			20X8		
31 Dec	Allowance for doubtful debts adjustment	168	1 Jan	Balance b/d	1,688
31 Dec	Balance c/d	1,520			
		1,688			1,688
			20X9		
			1 Jan	Balance b/d	1,520

CHAPTER 9 Bank reconciliations

1 (a) General ledger accounts:

		£	£
Debit	Sales ledger control account	9.00	
Credit	Bank account		9.00

(b) General ledger accounts:

		£	£
Debit	Bank charges account	15.80	
Credit	Bank account		15.80

(c) General ledger accounts:

		£	£
Debit	Gas expense account	300.00	
Credit	Bank account		300.00

(**Note** that if an analysed cash book is used and the postings are made to the general ledger from the totals of the analysis columns at the period end, the above amounts would be included in the totals and posted via the totals.)

2

Cash Receipts Book

Date	Details	£
4 March	J Killick	365.37 ✓
	D Francis	105.48 ✓
5 March	I Oliver	216.57 ✓
6 March	L Canter	104.78
7 March	R Trent	268.59
8 March	P Otter	441.78
		1,502.57

Cash Payments Book

Date	Details	Cheque number	£
4 March	L L Partners	002536	186.90 ✓
	P J Parler	002537	210.55 ✓
5 March	J K Properties	002538	500.00 ✓
	Harmer & Co	002539	104.78 ✓
	Plenith Ltd	002540	60.80
7 March	Wessex & Co	002541	389.40
8 March	Filmer Partners	002542	104.67
			1,557.10

Bank reconciliation statement at 1 March

	£	£
Balance per bank statement		835.68
Less: unpresented cheques		
002530	110.46 ✓	
002534	230.56 ✓	
002535	88.90 ✓	
		(429.92)
		405.76
Add: outstanding lodgement		102.45 ✓
Amended cash book balance		508.21

STATEMENT

first national
30 High Street
Benham
DR4 8TT

SOUTHFIELD ELECTRICAL LTD   **Account number:** 20-26-33 3126897

CHEQUE ACCOUNT   **Sheet 023**

Date		Paid out	Paid in	Balance
1 Mar	Balance b/f			835.68
4 Mar	Cheque No 002534	230.56✓		
	Credit		102.45✓	707.57
5 Mar	DD – National Telephones	145.00		
	Bank charges	7.80		554.77
6 Mar	Cheque No 002530	110.46✓		
	BACS JT Turner		486.20	930.51
7 Mar	Credit		470.85✓	
	Cheque No 002537	210.55✓		
	Cheque No 002536	186.90✓		
	Cheque No 002538	500.00✓		503.91
8 Mar	Cheque No 002535	88.90✓	✓	
	Credit		216.57	
	Cheque No 002539	104.78✓		526.80
8 Mar	Balance c/f			526.80

Bank account

	£		£
Balance b/d (from previous rec)	508.21	Payments	1,557.10
Receipts	1,502.57	Direct debit	145.00
BACS	486.20	Bank charges	7.80
		Balance c/d	787.08
	2,496.98		2,496.98
Balance b/d	787.08		

Bank reconciliation as at 8 March

	£
Balance per bank statement	526.80
Add outstanding lodgements:	
L Canter	104.78
R Trent	268.59
P Otter	441.78
Total to add:	815.15
Less unpresented cheques:	
002540	60.80
002541	389.40
002542	104.67
Total to subtract:	554.87
Balance as per cash book	787.08

CHAPTER 10   Control account reconciliations

1

Adjustment	Amount £	Debit (✓)	Credit (✓)
Undercast SDB	100	✓	
Sales returns	450		✓
Irrecoverable debt	210		✓

2

Adjustment	Amount £	Debit (✓)	Credit (✓)
PRDB overcast	300		✓
CPB overstated	270		✓
Discount	267	✓	

CHAPTER 11   **The trial balance, errors and the suspense account**

1

$$\text{Phone} = £3,400 + 300 \qquad = £3,700$$
$$\text{Insurance} = £1,600 - 200 \qquad = £1,400$$

CHAPTER 12 **The extended trial balance**

1   Open up a suspense account to record this difference.

2   Both a debit and a credit.

3   The closing inventory figure is a $\boxed{\text{credit entry}}$ in the statement of profit or loss columns and a $\boxed{\text{debit entry}}$ in the statement of financial position columns of the ETB.

INDEX

Notes

Notes

Notes

Notes

REVIEW FORM

How have you used this Text?
(Tick one box only)

☐ Home study

☐ On a course_____

☐ Other _____

Why did you decide to purchase this Text? *(Tick one box only)*

☐ Have used BPP Texts in the past

☐ Recommendation by friend/colleague

☐ Recommendation by a college lecturer

☐ Saw advertising

☐ Other _____

During the past six months do you recall seeing/receiving either of the following?
(Tick as many boxes as are relevant)

☐ Our advertisement in Accounting Technician

☐ Our Publishing Catalogue

Which (if any) aspects of our advertising do you think are useful?
(Tick as many boxes as are relevant)

☐ Prices and publication dates of new editions

☐ Information on Text content

☐ Details of our free online offering

☐ None of the above

Your ratings, comments and suggestions would be appreciated on the following areas of this Text.

	Very useful	Useful	Not useful
Introductory section	☐	☐	☐
Quality of explanations	☐	☐	☐
How it works	☐	☐	☐
Chapter tasks	☐	☐	☐
Chapter overviews	☐	☐	☐
Test your learning	☐	☐	☐
Index	☐	☐	☐

	Excellent	Good	Adequate	Poor
Overall opinion of this Text	☐	☐	☐	☐

Do you intend to continue using BPP Products? ☐ Yes ☐ No

Please note any further comments and suggestions/errors on the reverse of this page. The Head of Programme of this edition can be emailed at: nisarahmed@bpp.com

Please return to: Nisar Ahmed, AAT Head of Programme, BPP Learning Media Ltd, FREEPOST, London, W12 8AA.

REVIEW FORM (continued)

TELL US WHAT YOU THINK

Please note any further comments and suggestions/errors below